IN
REMEMBRANCE
OF
ME

IN
REMEMBRANCE
OF
ME

*A Manual
on Observing the
Lord's Supper*

JIM HENRY

BROADMAN
&HOLMAN
PUBLISHERS

Nashville, Tennessee

0-8054-2013-4

Published by Broadman & Holman Publishers, Nashville, Tennessee
Page Design and Typography by PerfecType, Nashville, Tennessee

Dewey Decimal Classification: 264.36
Subject Heading: LORD'S SUPPER
Library of Congress Card Catalog Number: 97-29356

Unless otherwise noted, Scripture quotations are from the Holy Bible, New
International Version, copyright © 1973, 1978, 1984 by International Bible
Society. NKJV, New King James Version, copyright © 1979, 1980, 1982,
Thomas Nelson, Inc., Publishers.

Library of Congress Cataloging-in-Publication Data
Henry, Jim, 1937-
    In remembrance of Me : a manual on observing the
Lord's Supper / Jim Henry.
        p.   cm.
Includes bibliographical references.
ISBN 0-8054-2013-4 (hardcover)
1. Lord's Supper (Liturgy)—Handbooks, manuals, etc.
2. Baptists—Liturgy—Handbooks, manuals, etc. I. Title.
BV825.5.H46 1998
264'.061036—dc21   97-29356
                                                                    CIP

02 5 4

Dedication

———— ❖ ————

This book is gratefully dedicated to the pastors and deacons with whom I have had the privilege to celebrate the Table and who have joined me in serving His people in this God-honoring, Jesus-exalting, Spirit-blessing experience around the cup and the bread. Their joy in participating has heightened my own joy and increased my anticipation of the marriage supper of the Lamb when our crucified, risen, and exalted Lord and Savior shall be the host. We will no longer "do this in remembrance," but in the reverence of worship in His eternal presence. *Soli Deo gloria*!

Contents

❖

Acknowledgments viii

Part 1
Chapter 1: The Foundation 3
Chapter 2: The Preparation 7
Chapter 3: The Implementation 11
Chapter 4: The Exhortation 15
Chapter 5: The Presentation 19
Chapter 6: The Invitation 25
Chapter 7: The Celebration 27

Part 2
Chapter 8: The Formulation 31
Chapter 9: The Proclamation 91
Chapter 10: The Illustration 153
Chapter 11: The Exaltation 177
Chapter 12: The Citation 185
Notes 197

Acknowledgments

———— ❖ ————

This book was born out of my own growing awareness of the importance of the powerful symbol of the Lord's Supper. It would not be a reality, however, without the contributions of some fellow pastors; the prayers and support of the staff, deacons, and community of believers at First Baptist Church, Orlando, Florida; the editing and expertise of Marilyn Jeffcoat, whose dedication to excellence is seen in these pages; and the faithfulness of my assistant, Sandi Mathis. I have sought to acknowledge all material, but in some cases, poor note-keeping and filing on my part has left some of the sources unknown. If per chance this includes a reader of this book, I trust you will overlook my inefficiency and allow me the privilege to take you to dinner as an expression of my gratitude!

Part 1

CHAPTER ONE

The Foundation

❖

F ar too often, the church has made the Lord's Supper a stepchild in the faith, a tag-on at the end of a service, a snapshot in the corner of a larger portrait. I as a pastor have been guilty of this. I am sure many other pastors join me in this confession.

Several years ago, during a sermon, I asked the question, "How many of you would like to observe the Lord's Supper more than once a quarter?" To my amazement nearly every hand went up in that large congregation. It registered with me that our people were hungry to share this symbol, and that they better understood its deeper significance than their pastor. This began a redirection in our emphasis on the Lord's Supper which has blessed our church—and me. It continues to be a growing and enriching experience in my journey of faith. And well it should. The celebration of the Table is deeply embedded in the fabric of our faith.

"The Lord's Supper" is the title given by Paul (1 Cor. 11:20). It bears other names. Luke used the phrase "breaking of bread" (Acts 2:42–46; 20:11; Luke 24:35). Paul employed the term *communion,* which referred to believers' relationship with the Lord (vertically) and with fellow believers (horizontally). *Eucharist,* another designation for the Lord's Supper, is derived from the Greek word *eucharistia,* "giving of thanks," as it implies the thanksgiving over the bread and wine (1 Cor. 11:24). Paul referred to it as "the Lord's table" (1 Cor. 10:21).

Augustine, in the fourth century A.D., called the Lord's Supper a "sacrament," which comes from a word that originally meant a pledge or bond. Many evangelicals have believed it is not a sacrament of saving grace, but it is rather a commitment, a promise, a pledge of allegiance to the Lord. The Gospels (Matt. 26:26–30; Mark 14:22–25; Luke 22:14–20) and Pauline accounts (1 Cor. 11:23) indicate that the Lord's Supper is rooted in the Old Testament ceremony of Passover.

Jesus used the occasion to identify Himself—by His actions and words—as the sacrificial Lamb, further expanding the messianic and eschatological meaning of the event. Christ's words and actions initiated the celebration of this powerful symbol, the early church practiced it (Acts 2:42, 20:7), and it continues to be observed as one of the most powerful symbols of the faith.

The Lord's Supper not only carries historical significance, but also theological significance in that it symbolizes the sacrificial death of our Lord Jesus. The bread and the wine symbolize the very body and blood of Christ. The blood, being essential to His earthly life and all other life, was shed redemptively for our lives.

The meal also carries ecclesiological significance for His body, the church. Wayne Grudem in his *Systematic Theology* has pointed out that the church reaps the benefits earned for us by His death and that we receive spiritual nourishment for our souls (John 6:53–57) through the Lord's Supper. The Table affirms His love to me in that He invites me to come to His supper, and my partaking of the meal affirms my faith in Him. I am redeemed and accepted by Christ's actions, and my actions proclaim it.[1]

The celebration of Communion also carries eschatological significance. As it commemorates a past event, it also anticipates a future consummation in His coming (1 Cor. 11:26). Thus, a feast of love, a memorial of faith, becomes a prophecy of hope.[2]

I invite you to join me in celebrating the Table, a dynamic symbol of the faith which foreshadows a future celebration when we will join Him at the wedding supper of the Lamb (Rev. 19:9). Celebrate the Table—and all its profound meaning—with new zeal and creative effort in your church. Let the believers in your congregation hear the command and the invitation to the Lord's Table.

> Come to this sacred table, not because
>   you must, but because you may;
> Come not to testify to your righteousness,
>   but that you sincerely love our Lord
>   Jesus Christ and desire to be His
>   true disciple;
> Come not because your goodness gives you
>   a right to come, but because in your
>   frailty and sin you stand in need of
>   heaven's mercy and help;

Come because you love the Lord a little
    and want to love Him more;
Come because He loved you and gave
    Himself for you;
Lift up your hearts, above your cares
    and fears;
Let this bread and wine be a sign of
    God's grace to you and a pledge of
    your love to the Lord Christ;
Receive the love of God and consecrate
    your life afresh to Christian obedience
    and service, to discover and do the
    will of God in humble faith.[3]

CHAPTER TWO

The Preparation

❖

As a bride prepares for her wedding or a salesperson works out a new presentation for an important client or a coach practices his team for the big game, so a minister should prepare for the celebration of the Lord's Table. Because of the high and holy nature of this event, all planning should be approached with creativity, thorough attention to detail, and excellence that befits the One being celebrated.

Through the years, I have found that my most able assistance in the preparation of the celebration has come through one of two sources: a *Lord's Supper ministry team* (or committee) and the *deacons* of the church. Those who assist in the preparation must have servants' hearts and the willingness to work behind the scenes. They must be led by someone with leadership and organizational skills. It is also of great importance that they are dependable.

The Lord's Supper ministry team must assume the responsibility of securing the elements. Our church uses grape juice and unleavened bread. The unleavened bread is prepared, packaged in 500-count pieces, and sold at Christian bookstores.

The team comes to the church the day before the service for preparations, if the supper is to be celebrated at a morning service. If it is to be observed at an evening service, it may be helpful for them to begin preparations the day before or prior to the morning worship, if it's scheduled on a Sunday. If your church is using silver trays or other pieces, these may first need polishing. If glass communion cups are being used, these may need to be checked for cleanliness. As an alternative to using the glass cups, many churches today are opting to use disposable plastic communion cups—for convenience and hygienic purposes.

The team then fills the cups and places the bread on the trays. The table and the elements are put in place, unless there is a morning service. (In that case, this can be done immediately after the morning service.)

Presentation of the elements is important. Placing the table on the platform gives it greater visibility and prominence in the service. This facilitates its being the focal point of worship. Draping the table with beautiful paraments or white linen cloths is appropriate for the presentation of this sacred meal. The elements may or may not be covered by a cloth. Our team chooses not to conceal the trays because of the visual ministry of these powerful symbols. Along with the trays, a beautiful chalice and plate (for a loaf of bread or larger wafer of unleavened bread) complete the presentation.

After the supper is observed, the presentation team begins the cleanup. In our church, this responsibility is delegated to a group of deacons and a team of men called *yokefellows* (assistants to our deacons who work with them in visitation, in caring for our members, and in preparing and serving the Lord's

Supper). All preparation, cleanup, and storage should be done in a designated area near the worship center (sanctuary). This room should have cabinets or closets that can be locked. It is also desirable to have a sink in this area. Here the trays can be emptied, cleaned, and stored. Table cloths or paraments should also be properly stored or cleaned. Unused juice and wafers should be stored or discarded. Used plastic cups should be picked up and thrown away.

CHAPTER THREE

The Implementation

———— ❖ ————

When talking with fellow pastors, I am often asked about the method of observance of the Lord's Supper in our church. I, too, seek similar information in an attempt to keep our coming to His table fresh and meaningful. The following are some of the most frequently posed questions concerning this holy meal.

1. When do you serve the Lord's Table?

In my first years of ministry, I thought the Lord's Supper could be served only once a quarter and in a church sanctuary. The passing years, however, have widened my horizons considerably on the "when" of the table. As I mentioned in the first chapter, some years ago our congregation increased its emphasis on this meal in the life of our body of believers. We began observing the table ten to eleven times a year, usually in the evening worship hour. Also, at least once a year, we celebrate the table during the Sunday morning worship service—to meet the needs of the elderly, those who work in the evenings, and others who attend only morning worship.

I realize some congregations do not have a regular evening worship service, so our system may not work for them. If this were true for our church, I would still observe it every month—during the morning worship service.

In my earlier years, I was guilty of tagging the Lord's Supper on to the end of everything else we did, including a full-length message. I have since repented! The Lord's Supper is so important and dramatic that we have made it the apex of our Sunday evening worship services, observing it once a month. We incorporate baptisms and parent/baby dedications in this service, calling it our Celebration Service. It is a service of praise, which begins with baptisms, followed by parents dedicating themselves to raise their infants in the Christian faith, and climaxed by the Lord's Supper.

2. When and where is it appropriate to serve the Lord's Table beyond the local church assembly?

There are times and places "outside the walls" that are not only appropriate but ideal for this meaningful worship experience. For instance, if a church group is away on a retreat, renewal weekend, or trip with church leaders or a minister present, and the church gives permission, sharing the table can be unforgettable.

I have found this especially gratifying with groups visiting the Holy Land and observing the Lord's Supper at the Garden Tomb, by the Sea of Galilee, or on the Mount of Olives, while overlooking Jerusalem at night. The experience of sharing this sacred meal, reading the account of our Lord's suffering, and singing "The Old Rugged Cross" in that setting leaves few dry eyes and great lifelong memories.

3. Should the Lord's Supper be served outside of group settings?

Our church makes arrangements to carry the Lord's Supper to the houses of our shut-ins at least once a year. If we have hospitalized members who request to observe communion, we make it possible.

4. Should communion be shared at weddings?

There is certainly no prohibition against this, but I have found it difficult to do for a number of reasons. If the bride and groom wish to participate, it is necessary for us to consider their wedding party and guests. It may put some people from other religious groups or those who have no personal commitment to Jesus Christ on the spot. This may leave out some—or many. As I believe a wedding is a "community affair," this may not be advisable. There is also the matter of preparing and serving the elements, as well as the time factor. All things being considered, a wedding may not be the best time or place to administer the table.

5. What are some other special times in the life of the church for the Lord's Supper?

A gratifying occasion to share the Lord's Supper is to plan a church fellowship dinner. After partaking of the elements in this less formal setting, the people would remain around their tables and enjoy a meal. This experience builds friendship and ties into the practices of the early New Testament church.

Another meaningful experience is the first communion experience of those recently baptized. Seats may be reserved in the front of the church for these new recipients. They may be served with a glass or olive wood cup that they may take with them as a keepsake of this important occasion. After the service, a receiving line can be formed, and the congregation can welcome these new members into the church family.

CHAPTER FOUR

The Exhortation

— ❖ —

For worshipers to receive the highest blessing from the table, a certain amount of spiritual preparation is necessary. Many come to the table with a thousand other things on their minds. Attitudes and hearts have to be readjusted. The music, message, testimonies, Scripture readings, responsive readings, and vignettes are valuable means by which to reach worship goals.

But I believe we need to take our preparation a step further. It is important to take several minutes in the service to address some other key matters. I do not deal with every issue each time we share the Lord's Supper, but over the course of three or four table occasions, each is addressed. I have found five things about which people either have questions or need instruction in order to facilitate a positive communion experience:

1. Who is "eligible" to participate in this sacred feast?

In today's diverse society, with many people coming to our churches from different denominational or nondenominational backgrounds, the question often arises, "Am I welcome to participate in this church?" An explanation of your church's or denomination's position will immediately set them at ease.

2. Am I "worthy" to take of the bread and cup?

Through the years I have found several people refusing to take of the table because they feel some past sin disqualifies them. I have also found some of such humble spirit that even the slightest thought or attitude that is not Christlike is cause for them to refuse participation. At other times the uncertainty of the meaning of 1 Corinthians 11:27–30 has brought confusion. A few words of interpretation of this passage and clarification can be helpful.

3. How can I approach the table with unconfessed sin?

I give a time for the confession of sin by persons in the privacy of their hearts. I explain how important it is for us to approach this holy time with our being "clean" before the Lord. I allow a minute or so with no words or music, just our being quiet before the Lord. This time of silent introspection and confession is concluded with a pastoral prayer of corporate confession of sin and an expression of gratitude for forgiveness.

4. Should I partake of the Lord's Supper when I am not at peace with my neighbor?

To address this, I open the door for anyone to go to someone in the fellowship whom they have wronged or have ill feelings toward (and vice versa) and ask forgiveness. On one occasion, I personally felt compelled by the Holy Spirit to approach one of our deacons who would be serving the people with me and ask his forgiveness. (How could I ask the people to do what I was unwilling to do?) The deacon was gratified and surprised. The result has been a deepening friendship through the years.

5. Should those visiting with us share this meal?

I make allowance for those who may be visiting with family or friends, for newcomers, for God-seekers, and for members of other denominations or religions by saying:

> We are always pleased and privileged to have guests. We realize you may not wish to observe this marvelous symbol of our faith with us. Feel free to watch, listen, and pass the elements to those beside you. We honor your decision and are delighted you are with us for this sacred meal. Perhaps what you may experience will raise questions that need further explanation. After the service, please come to me or to one of our pastors, and we will be glad to talk with you.

This is done before we serve the bread and cup, and sometimes you can almost hear the sighs of relief by those whose concerns have been addressed. It is important that we not take for granted that all those present are knowledgeable or fully prepared to enter into this awesome experience of recognizing the Lordship of Jesus Christ.

CHAPTER FIVE

The Presentation

❖

O ur church has several ways of serving the elements. The more traditional way calls for the deacons to sit together in the front rows at the beginning of the worship service. When I have finished the worship time to prepare the people for receiving the elements, I have the deacons stand in a line across the front of the worship center, facing the elements. The associate pastor stands at one end of the table, and I stand at the other. We remove the covers from the trays and have assistant pastors or deacon officers assist us in giving trays to our deacons for distribution of the elements to the congregation. Once all trays are in the deacons' hands, I nod my head and they begin to serve. I sit down, along with the others who have assisted me, to pray and meditate.

At least two weeks prior to communion, our deacons are assigned their given areas of the church to serve. (If for some reason they are unable to attend, it is their responsibility to secure a substitute or call a deacon officer for assistance.) During the service, the deacons go to their designated areas and begin serving the people. After they finish serving, they go to the back of the worship center.

When all have been served, the deacons come forward together and remain standing. They return their trays. When all trays have been collected, I take two trays and give one to a deacon officer, usually the chairman. The assistant pastor does the same. The assistant pastor and I begin at the middle of the line and serve to the flanks, meeting the officers who have started at the flanks and moved toward the center. When we meet, I take his tray and serve the deacon leader. The assistant pastor serves the other deacon officer. Moving to the platform, the assistant pastor and I serve each other.

As I serve the deacons and assistant pastor, I usually look them in the eye and speak to each one. I use expressions such as

- "His blood shed for us . . ."
- "Jesus paid it all . . ."
- "God so loved us, He gave His Son . . ."
- "His body given for us . . ."
- "The greatest love in all the world . . ."
- "Jesus loves you, and I love you . . ."
- "Such love . . ."
- "Broken and spilled out for us . . ."

I have found these moments some of the most meaningful experiences in my ministry. They build unifying bonds of fellowship with our spiritual leaders. (I use this method with both the bread and the cup.)

When the deacons and pastor have been served, I face the congregation with a large piece of unleavened bread. How large? Large enough to be seen to the back row of our large church. I hold it up high and make a comment such as this:

> On the night in which the hinges of history turned so decisively, our Lord met with those whom He had devoted the very essence of His life and mission. They did not understand the impact of His mission nor His profound love for them. As He, only thirty-three years of age, looked into those eyes reflecting the light of the oil lamps, He said, "This is my body, given for you."

At this point, with the bread held high, I break it slowly and deliberately and say, "Take. Eat."

I bow my head and breathe a quiet but audible prayer such as this:

> Lord Jesus, thank You for loving us with such love that You would be wounded for our transgressions and bruised for our iniquities. We cannot comprehend it, nor do we deserve it, but we are eternally grateful.

I repeat this process with the cup. The cup I use is a large silver-plated goblet. I used to use a small cup like our members use, but I switched to the larger goblet so all can see this important symbol. When I take the cup, I lift it up as I did the bread. I have noticed that this small change has dramatically increased the effectiveness of the presentation.

After I drink from the cup and pray, the deacons move away from the altar area to allow room for people to respond to the invitation and time of renewal (see chapter 6, "The Invitation").

A second method of serving the Lord's Supper our church uses as a time-saver is what we call "fast track." It in no way lessens the impact of the service, but it saves seven to ten minutes we may want to capture for extra time in praise and worship, preaching, drama, or praying.

When we utilize the fast track, our deacons meet at the rear of the worship center, where the trays of bread and cups of juice have been placed. We still keep a large table on the platform at the front with the goblet and a tray present, again for the visual, symbolic presence. As I make my opening remarks, the deacons get their trays and, at my signal, come forward to serve. When they have finished, they return to the back and are served by fellow deacons or assistant pastors.

A third method we employ is the placing of several tables of the elements in key places throughout our worship center. We encourage our people to sit together as families or with special friends in Christ. We post deacons behind the tables. After I give instructions to the people, they come forward and are served by the deacons. As the pastors or deacons step forward, we have a brief special prayer for the people as they kneel. They return to their seats and meditate while others are receiving the elements.

This has proven to be a very popular and powerful way of celebrating the table in our church. (NOTE: These areas may be designated by banners. Behind each table is placed a banner with a Christian symbol or term. Worshipers choose to commune where a banner communicates their thoughts in worship. See chap. 8, Service 3 for a "banner service.")

In order to increase congregational participation, I have used several things that help pull the people into active rather than passive observation:

- As the people receive the elements, encourage them to bow their heads and contemplate the Cross—remembering when they came to faith, what it cost for them to be saved, the scene at the Crucifixion, the joy of forgiveness.

- Invite someone or several people to share their most meaningful experience(s) in observing the table with the entire congregation. This can be accomplished by enlisting them beforehand, or it can be spontaneous.

- Have individuals turn to the people beside them prior to their taking of the elements and say, "His body given for you and me . . ." or "His blood paid for my sins . . ."

- Hand out one large nail to each person seated next to the aisle or each row. Before a nail is passed down a row, the terrible nature of the physical Crucifixion is addressed from the pulpit. As the nail is passed, instruct each person to hold the nail for a moment and think of what Jesus suffered for his or her sake.

- Sing the great hymns of the faith or praise songs that relate to the Cross, the blood, or the Lord's Supper. The music should be familiar, or project the words so there is no fumbling with hymnals or printed song sheets. Our music director usually remains seated and leads the congregation from that position in order to keep the focus off of him. The songs may be sung a cappella or accompanied by the piano, organ, or synthesizer. An ensemble or choir may lead the singing for another variation.

CHAPTER SIX

The Invitation

❖

One can scarcely enter into the Lord's Supper without being touched spiritually, emotionally, and intellectually. This often stirs a desire to make some kind of response to the Holy Spirit's quickening of hearts. I believe it is necessary always to provide an opportunity for people to respond—privately and publicly. My practice is to have everyone stand with heads bowed and praise the Lord for His grace in our lives and for the fresh touch we have experienced.

I then speak to those present who have never made that most important of all decisions—the decision to accept Christ. I explain briefly God's plan of salvation. This is followed by an invitation for those who desire to accept Jesus as Savior and Lord to pray quietly a simple, directed prayer of faith:

Dear Lord Jesus, I have been reminded of my sin and the cost to satisfy that sin. I know I cannot save myself. I confess my sin, and I ask You to forgive me. I receive You now as my personal Savior and Lord. I trust You— and You alone—to save me. Please help me live for You and become like You, as I live the rest of my life. Thank

You for shedding your blood for my salvation. I love You. In Jesus' name, Amen.

With heads of the worshipers still bowed, I invite those who prayed with me to come forward, so they may be assisted in taking their next steps in the faith. I also invite those who have accepted Christ previously but have not confessed Him in baptism and church membership to come forward. I ask others who want to become a part of our church family by the transfer of membership or who want to come to the altar to pray and renew their vows to Jesus to feel free to do so. As I lead in prayer, the instruments play. The music continues as the church prays and the people respond.

It is amazing to witness what God does in these moments of invitation that follow communion. Since we began emphasizing the Lord's Table thirteen years ago by making it central to the worship experience, we have never had a communion service without a public response—and sometimes in double digits! I strongly encourage churches to incorporate a time of invitation for private and public response to the work of the Holy Spirit.

CHAPTER SEVEN

The Celebration

❖

A s I wrap up a tremendous service, I desire to send people away celebrating the continuing power and ministry of the living Christ in their lives. I do so by spending a brief time recapping the positive things that have taken place in the service: the baptisms, the missionaries we commissioned, the safe return of our students from camp, someone's loved ones being saved, the people who joined our fellowship, the generous offering, etc. We also focus briefly on the sense of oneness we have felt as God's family at the table.

These closing celebration moments are preceded by a love offering, which is over and above our regular offering. This offering is usually designated to assist those in our fellowship having financial challenges because of layoffs, health problems, marital discord, or other circumstances. We administer the funds received through our pastoral and deacon offices. Through the years this offering has generated hundreds of thousands of dollars to help our people in a discreet way. It has made survival possible for many people and has enabled us to show the world that we do look after our own. The letters and the words of appreciation we have received are reminders that this is a worthy and Christlike thing to do.

To conclude the service, I usually have the people join hands with their neighbors, as the lights in the sanctuary are darkened, and we sing a song of victory, joy, and gratitude (such as "Victory In Jesus," "Amazing Grace," or "How Great Thou Art"). This further links us with the experience of Jesus and His disciples after they observed the Passover and inaugurated the Lord's Supper: "When they had sung a hymn, they went out to the Mount of Olives" (Matt. 26:30; Mark 14:26).

More than likely, the songs of Jesus' disciples came from the hymns of praise, trust, and thanksgiving found in Psalms 115 through 118. These can be used in services today by having all or a part of one of these songs read prior to the final song and benediction or read alone as an ending in itself. After we sing, I usually pronounce a brief prayer of blessing on the people as we leave to carry out our mission in the world.

As the congregation is dismissed, they are encouraged to extend Christ's love to others through a handshake or hug as they depart. Also, we use our fellowship hall and its kitchen facilities on Sunday evenings by inviting our people, their family, friends, and guests to join us for a time of fellowship and food. This invitation is always met with a hearty response!

There's one other thing I have noticed: After the dismissal, the people continue to stand around, talking and laughing—sometimes for an hour or more after the final "amen." The unifying effect of the Lord's Table is more penetrating and healthy for the body life of the church than I could have imagined when I first began to underscore the centrality of the Lord's Table.

Part 2

CHAPTER EIGHT

The Formulation

❖ ───────

For most pastors and worship leaders, bringing a fresh approach to observing the Lord's Table is a constant challenge. The fast pace of today's society, coupled with the increasing demands on church leaders, makes it difficult to plan and reflect on the most inspiring way to obey our Lord's command, "Do this in remembrance of me."

Following are orders of worship, including drama and music, which you may use as outlined. Or, you can use selected ideas from several services to formulate your own or simply use them as a vehicle to stir the creative juices. There is one thing of which you can be sure: your efforts in preparation will bring a freshness in your approach to the table, which will yield a new vitality and anticipation of the Lord's Supper. It will also increase awareness of the meal's power, which, in turn, will probably prompt greater participation as the people seek the benefits of His supper.

Service 1:
General/Lenten/Maundy Thursday

ORGAN PRELUDE

BAPTISM

CALL TO WORSHIP
    Praise Team: *Everlasting Hope* (B-flat)

SONGS OF PRAISE
    Nothing but the Blood of Jesus (vv. 1, 2 in G; v. 4 in A-flat)
    Glory to His Name (v. 1 in A-flat; v. 4 in A)
    Because He Lives (chorus only in A)

WORSHIP IN GIVING

LORD'S SUPPER
    "The Living Lord's Supper"
    Sharing of the Word
["Basin Behavior"; see instructions on p. 22]

Reenactment of the Lord's Supper
  • [Disciples, one or two at a time, enter to greet Jesus and take their place at the table.]

  • [Jesus speaks to the disciples and then gets up from the table and begins to wash their feet at stage right.]

  • [Jesus returns to the table and blesses the bread and serves it. He then blesses the wine and serves it. Congregation takes the elements with the disciples at the same time.]

- [Following the Lord's Supper, the disciples, again one or two at a time, exit, leaving Jesus alone—praying at center of the table. Lights fade and music leader directs congregational singing of closing hymn.]

Sharing of the Elements
Instrumental and Vocal: *There Is a Redeemer* (D–E-flat)
[As disciples enter]

Congregation: *Grace Greater Than Our Sin* (G)
[As disciples enter; during footwashing]

Vocal: *How Beautiful* (Pageant Music)
[As elements are served]

Vocal and Congregation: *O the Blood of Jesus* (F)
[After elements are served]

HYMN OF INVITATION
O How He Loves You and Me (A-flat)

BENEDICTION
No Other Name (C–D-flat)

Basin Behavior
This is a reenactment of the Lord's Supper with actors, in full costume, portraying the disciples and with the stage set as the Upper Room. Along with the table for the Lord's Supper, which is at center stage, there should be a single basin of water at the end of the table on stage right. At the end of stage left, outside of the Lord's Supper scene, there should be another basin of water on a pedestal, lit by a single spotlight.

NOTE: The elements should be passed out to the congregation as they enter the worship service. Christian bookstores stock individual cartons containing one serving of juice and bread.

The minister should tell this story as a narrative, rather than read the following Scripture references: John 13:1–17; Matthew 27:20–24; Luke 22:7–20. He walks into the scene following the offering and, in casual narrative, tells the congregation that in just a moment they will see the beautiful reenactment of the Last Supper of Christ and His disciples. Before this takes place, however, the minister should direct the congregation to note two basins of water on either side of the stage: one on the floor and one on a pedestal. These represent two views worshipers have at this Supper:

> The first view is that of Pilate, who would go to a basin and, after his complete examination of Jesus Christ and with full knowledge of Christ's innocence, say, "I wash my hands of Him." Some who join us in this service today say with their lives, "I want nothing to do with this One who is called Christ." You, like Pilate, know about Him, know that He is the Son of God, know that He is the Savior of the world, know that He died for your sins, know that He was resurrected on the third day, and know that He *lives* today. Yet, like Pilate, you say to the world, "I wash my hands of this man."

> The other view is that of a servant, emulating the example of Jesus. You who have accepted Christ as Lord and Savior of your life will want to follow Him.

Following Him means taking upon yourself the humility and servanthood of one who stoops to wash the feet of another. The picture of Jesus washing the feet of His disciples at the Passover meal is vital in that He told Peter, "You don't need to be washed all over, but you do need to be clean." For those of us who gather now at the Lord's Table, we, as true believers of our Lord, need not salvation, but sanctification, cleansing, and forgiveness of our sins before we take this meal.

NOTE: At this point, the minister should draw the obvious distinction between the two basin behaviors and tell the congregation they cannot escape the fact that they—by their beliefs, attitudes, actions, and commitment—fall into one of these two categories represented by the basins. Each person will either submit to the Lord—humbly seeking a servant's heart and following Christ's example—or respond as Pilate—pridefully washing hands of the influence and Lordship of Christ. The minister should then lead the congregation in a twofold invitation: (1) to humbly accept the free gift of God's grace through salvation in Jesus Christ, and (2) to ask the Holy Spirit to convict the believer of sin and to prepare the believer to join "Christ and His disciples" at His table.

Following the invitation, the minister should inform the congregation that it is almost time for the actors portraying the disciples and Christ to enter. He instructs them to take the elements as instructed by the actor portraying Christ. The congregation should be informed that there will be no further instructions given. They are now to become a part of the Lord's Supper.

At the conclusion of the Lord's Supper, the music leader should come to the platform and lead the congregation in the singing of the closing hymn. This concludes the service.

Contributed by Larry L. Thompson
First Baptist Church, Ft. Lauderdale, Florida

Service 2:
General

CALL TO WORSHIP

Prelude

Opportunities of Ministry

Call to Prayer

Meditation: *This Do Ye*

WORSHIP THROUGH SONG

Hymn: *O For a Thousand Tongues to Sing*

Welcome of Guests

Fellowship Song: *One in the Bond of Love*

WORSHIP THROUGH GIVING

Offertory Hymn: *Love Divine, All Loves Excelling*

Offertory

WORSHIP THROUGH OBEDIENCE
The Observance of the Lord's Supper

Bearing the Cross
Must Jesus Bear the Cross Alone

On the Cross
The Old Rugged Cross

Beneath the Cross
Beneath the Cross

By the Cross
Jesus, Keep Me Near the Cross

Above the Cross
Man of Sorrows, What a Name

Invitation: *When I Survey the Wondrous Cross*

The Serving of the Bread: *In Remembrance*

The Serving of the Fruit of the Vine: *I Eat This Bread, Alleluia!*

Receiving New Members

United in the Cross
Blest Be the Tie That Binds

BENEDICTION

POSTLUDE

Contributed by Roy T. Edgemon, Director, Director, Discipleship and Family Development Division, Baptist Sunday School Board, Nashville, Tennessee

Service 3:
General/Banners/Contemporary

PRESERVICE
(Live band or instrumental CD/cassette)

[The following banner package should be tied together instrumentally with no break in the music. Keyboard, guitar, etc., should fill under all segues using these times to transition to the next song.]

Introduction over first song
Just as the sons of Israel identified themselves by raising their families' banners high over their tents, we come now in worship to identify ourselves with Jesus Christ . . . to lift high the Lord, our Banner!
Lift High the Lord Our Banner (all, 2 times)

WORSHIP PACKAGE
[Banners enter during the preceding song, joining the others arranged at the front, facing the people. Following the Scripture for each banner, as the corresponding song is sung, that particular banner should move to its appropriate place in the room.]

1. Scripture: "He who is the blessed and only Potentate, the King of kings and Lord of lords . . . to [Him] be honor and everlasting power" (1 Tim. 6:15–16, NKJV).
Banner: "King of kings and Lord of lords"
Song: *King of Kings* (all, 2 times, 2nd time in higher key with full band)

2. Scripture: "Jesus spoke to them again saying, 'I am the light of the world. He who follows Me shall not walk in darkness, but have the light of life'" (John 8:12, NKJV).

Banner: "Light of the World"

Song: *Everlasting Light* (all, 2 times with full band)

3. Scripture: "Jesus said to her, 'I am the resurrection and the life. He who believes in Me, though he may die, shall live. And whoever lives and believes in Me shall never die'" (John 11:25–26, NKJV).

Banner: "The Resurrection and the Life"

Song: *My Life Is in You, Lord* (all on chorus, solo v., all on chorus with full band)

4. Scripture: "'The Redeemer will come to Zion, / And to those who turn from transgression in Jacob,' says the LORD" (Isa. 59:20, NKJV).

Banner: "Redeemer"

Song: *There Is a Redeemer* (solo on v. 1 beginning "There is a Redeemer," then all join on chorus with keyboard or guitar only; solo on v. 2 beginning "Jesus, My Redeemer," then all join on chorus)

5. Scripture: "John saw Jesus coming toward him, and said, 'Behold! The Lamb of God who takes away the sin of the world!'" (John 1:29, NKJV).

Banner: "Lamb of God"

Song: *Glory to the Lamb* (solo 1 time, then all, 1 time with keyboard or guitar only)

6. Scripture: "He is despised and rejected by men, / A Man of sorrows and acquainted with grief. / And we hid, as it

were our faces from Him; / He was despised, and we did
not esteem Him / Surely He has borne our griefs" (Isa.
53:3–4a, NKJV).

Banner: "Man of Sorrows"

Song: *Man of Sorrows* (solo on v. 1 beginning "Man of
Sorrows," then all on v. 2 beginning "Bearing shame" with
keyboard or guitar only)

Transition

Let's worship together the One who paid the price for
each of us . . . the only One who is worthy of our praise.

You Are Worthy to Be Praised (several times in ascending
keys)
Oh, How I Love Jesus (several times)
I Exalt Thee (several times in 2 keys)

MESSAGE

"The Banner of the Cross"

THE LORD'S SUPPER

The Elements

[People should be instructed during the message to pick a banner that means something special to them. The banners will be
spread out across the room with both elements at the foot of
each banner. There should be room at each banner for people
to receive the elements from the minister or deacon officiating
at the banner and to kneel and pray for a moment. At the conclusion of the message, the pastor will let people know it is time
for them to move to "their" banner at their leisure. The time
should be relaxed and, by all means, not rushed. Acoustic guitar
(piano if guitar is not available) should play under this time

with a package of songs, choruses, and hymns suitable to this observance.]

INVITATION
In My Life, Lord, Be Glorified

BENEVOLENCE OFFERING
Band: *Jesus Is the Answer*

CLOSING SONG
Congregation: *Jesus Is the Answer*

POSTSERVICE
(Live band or CD/cassette)

NOTE: A praise/worship team of singers should be used to lead this type of worship. All hymns used above should be done in an updated/current style with alternate harmonies, rhythms, meters, etc. Many alternate harmonizations are available in chorus/song books by such companies as Integrity, Maranatha, Word, Prism, Benson, etc. Anthem arrangements will also often work well. Many collections that offer contemporary medleys for worship are currently available.

Contributed by David Taylor
First Baptist Church, Orlando, Florida

Service 4:
General/Lenten/Drama

NOTE: The following is not a complete order of worship. It is a dramatic reading to be used during the serving of the elements.

LORD'S SUPPER
Scripture Interpretation
[Directions: Four voices, characters unseen, from the balcony (as the first element is served)]:

V1: Jesus Christ. *[Pause]* Jesus Christ.

V2: Alpha.

V3: Ancient of Days.

V4: Beginning. Beloved Son.

V3: Sovereign. God.

V1: Immanuel, God with us. King of Glory.

V2: *[Strong]* Lion of the Tribe of Judah!

V3: *[Quiet]* Lamb of God.

V2: *[Strong]* Cornerstone! Commander!

V3: *[Pause]* Sacrifice. *[Pause]*

V4: So they delivered Him to be crucified to the place, Golgotha, which is translated, "the Place of the Skull." His wounded body was nailed to a cross.

V1: *[Pause]* As He was dying, the soldiers divided His garments among themselves, casting lots for them. *[Matter-of-factly]* It was the third hour when they crucified Him. And the inscription of the charge against Him, nailed above his head read: THE KING OF THE JEWS.

V4: And they crucified two robbers with Him.

V1: Those passing by were hurling insults at Him, wagging their heads and saying:

V3: *[Dramatically]* "Ha! You who are going to destroy the temple and rebuild it in three days, save Yourself. Come down from the cross!!" *[Additional vocal grumbling is heard.]*

V1: In the same manner the chief priest along with the scribes, were mocking Him:

V2: *[In character]* "He saved others, but He cannot save Himself! *[Additional voices again.]* Let this Christ, the King of the Jews come down, so that we may see and believe.

V1: And those who were crucified with Him were casting the same insults at Him. *[Pause]* When the sixth hour had come, darkness fell over the whole land until the ninth hour."

V2: Jesus Christ.

V3: The Lamb of God . . .

V4: . . . Who takes away the sins of the world.

V1: *[Quietly]* But . . . they did not know.

V2: "For God so loved the world that He gave His only begotten Son, Jesus."

BREAK BETWEEN SERVING OF ELEMENTS

[As the second element is served]:

V4: Jesus Christ.

V3: Mediator. Messenger of the Covenant.

V2: Salvation. Source of Eternal Salvation.

V1: Image of God. *[Pause]*

V4: *[Pause]* And at the ninth hour Jesus cried out with a loud voice:

V3: "My God, My God, why hast Thou forsaken Me?"

V2: He cried out again:

V3: "It is finished!" *[Pause]* And, Jesus breathed His last.

V1: And, one of the soldiers pierced His side, and out came blood and water.

V4: "He was a man of sorrows and acquainted with grief. And our sorrows He carried. He was pierced through for our transgressions and crushed for our iniquities; by His scourging we are healed . . .

V2: . . . He was afflicted, yet He did not open His mouth. . . . Like a lamb to slaughter and like a sheep silent before its shearers, He Himself bore our sins."

V3: "God so loved the world that He gave his only begotten Son, that whosoever believes in Him shall not perish but have everlasting life."

V1: Jesus. Redeemer.

V2: Jesus. Spotless. Innocent. Just.

V3: Christ. Perfector of our faith.

V4: Jesus Christ. Victor. Our Savior.

Contributed by R. Wayne Johnson
First Baptist Church, Orlando, Florida

Service 5:
General

NOTE: The following worship format is only the communion portion of a worship service. Worship planners may incorporate this as a part of other service material.

[Those serving communion should come forward at this time.]
Minister One:
Almighty God, to You all hearts are open, all desires known, and from You no secrets are hidden. Cleanse the thoughts of our hearts by the inspiration of Your Holy Spirit, that we may perfectly love You and worthily magnify Your holy name through Christ our Lord.

Most merciful God, we confess that we have sinned against You in thought, word, and deed, by what we have done, and by what we have left undone. We have not loved You with our whole heart. We have not loved our neighbors as ourselves. We are truly sorry, and we humbly repent. For the sake of Your Son, Jesus Christ, have mercy on us and forgive us that we may delight in Your will and walk in Your ways to the glory of Your name. Amen.

Choir: *God's Sacrifice**
[Communion elements should be distributed at this time.]

Minister Two
[Leads choir and congregation in the Apostles' Creed]:

Let us affirm our common statement of faith as the apostles proclaimed:

> *I believe in God the Father, Almighty, Creator of heaven and Earth; And in Jesus Christ, His only Son, our Lord: Who was conceived by the Holy Spirit, born of the Virgin Mary, suffered under Pontius Pilate, was crucified, died, and buried. He descended into Hell. The third day He rose again from the dead; He ascended into Heaven and sitteth at the right hand of God, the Father Almighty; From thence He shall come to judge the quick and the dead. I believe in the Holy Spirit, the Holy Christian Church, the communion of saints, the forgiveness of sins, the resurrection of the body, and the life everlasting. Amen.*

Minister One:

In God's infinite love He made us for Himself; and, when we fell into sin and became subject to evil and death, He, in His mercy, sent Jesus Christ, His only Son, to share our human nature, to live and die as one of us, to reconcile us unto Himself. He stretched out His arms upon the cruel cross at Calvary and offered Himself, in obedience to the will of God, a perfect sacrifice for the whole world. Then came the day of Unleavened Bread on which the Passover lamb had to be sacrificed. Jesus sent Peter and John, saying, "Go and make preparations for us to eat the Passover." "Where do you want us to prepare for it?" they asked. He replied, "As you enter the city, a man carrying a jar of water will meet you. Follow him to the house that he enters, and say to the owner of the house, 'The Teacher asks: Where is the guest room, where I may eat the Passover with my disciples?' He will show you a large upper room all furnished. Make preparations there."

They left and found things just as Jesus had told them. So they prepared the Passover. When the hour came, Jesus and His apostles reclined at the table. And He said to them, "I have eagerly desired to eat this Passover with you before my sufferings begin. For I tell you, I will not eat again until it finds fulfillment in the kingdom of God." After taking the cup, he gave thanks and said, "Take this and divide it among you. For I tell you I will not drink again of the fruit of the vine until the kingdom of God comes."

*And he took the bread, gave thanks and broke it, and gave it to them, saying, "This is my body given for you; do this in remembrance of me." *[The congregation will partake of the bread together.]*

In the same way, after the supper he took the cup, saying, "This cup is the new covenant in my blood, which is poured out for you." *[The congregation will partake of the cup together.]*

Congregational Singing *(celebration/exaltation songs)*

*From Christ Church Choir's recording *Our God Is Lifted Up*, available in Christian bookstores.

Contributed by L. H. Hardwick, Jr.
Christ Church, Nashville, Tennessee

Service 6:
General

NOTE: The following should be printed on the front page of the worship bulletin and/or displayed on a screen and used during the "Symphony and Praise" segment of this service.

Symphony of Praise

Joy
Rest
Help
Peace
Father
Worthy
Anchor
Refuge
Merciful
Strength
Almighty
Provider
Sustainer
Sufficient
Comforter
Mighty One
All Knowing
King of Glory
Prince of Life
Unspeakable
Alpha and Omega

King of kings
Lamb of God
Foundation
Cornerstone
Redeemer
Sovereign
Liberator
Holy One
Sacrifice
Fortress
Creator
Eternal
Master
Friend
Hope
Love
Life

PRELUDE

INVOCATION

PRAISE MEDLEY
I Will Celebrate (3 times in E; solo: 1 time in E, 1 time in F)
The Name of the Lord (1 time in F, 1 time in G)

SYMPHONY OF PRAISE *(spoken)*
[Can also be used as close of service. Printed names must be available in bulletin, on screen, etc. Worship leader introduces and leads. Congregation reads together. When a blank in the copy appears, each worshiper inserts the description or name of praise he selects.**]

Leader:
We Will Speak His Praises!

Leader and Congregation:
Lord, I praise you because you are my SAVIOR.
I praise you because you are AWESOME!
I praise you because you are PERFECT.
God, I thank you because you are my _____.**
God, I thank you because you are _____.**

I praise you because you LOVE ME!
I praise you because you are my FORTRESS!
I praise you because you are _____.**
I praise you because today you are my _____.**

I praise you because you are the MAJESTIC ONE!
I praise you because you are the RIGHTEOUS ONE!
God, I praise you because you are my _____.**
God, I praise you because you ... ARE!!

Lord, I worship you because you are my SAVIOR.
I worship you because you are _____.**
I worship you because you are PERFECT.

God, I thank you because you are the _____.**
God, I thank you because you LOVE me!
God, I praise you because you ... ARE!!

WORSHIP PACKAGE
  'Tis So Sweet to Trust in Jesus (1 time in G)
  I Have Decided to Follow Jesus (1 time in C, 1 time in E-flat)
  Glorify Thy Name (1 time in B-flat)

Transition

"At the name of Jesus, every knee shall bow and every tongue confess that Jesus Christ is Lord."

There's Something About That Name (1 time in E-flat)

Jesus, Draw Me Close (1 time in F, 1 time in G)

WELCOME/OFFERTORY PRAYER

OFFERTORY SOLO

Vocal ensemble: *We Shall Wear a Crown*

SCRIPTURE

John 12:32–33

THE MEDITATION

"Universal Magnetism" [see chap. 9, Sermon 3]

THE LORD'S SUPPER

Bread

Piano: *Let Us Break Bread Together on Our Knees*

Cup

Flugal horn: *In This Very Room*

INVITATION

Piano/Synthesizer/Vocals: *Open Our Eyes, Lord*

CLOSING REMARKS

POSTLUDE

Contributed by worship team of Ragan M. Vandegriff III, David Taylor, Mr. Terry Winch, R. Wayne Johnson First Baptist Church, Orlando, Florida

Service 7:
Contemporary/General

PRESERVICE
(Live band or instrumental CD/cassette)

Introduction over first song
We come together to lift high the name of Jesus. Lift Him up!

WORSHIP PACKAGE
Lord, I Lift Your Name on High (verse, chorus, verse, chorus, chorus)

My Life Is in You, Lord (2 times chorus, verse solo, 2 times chorus)

Transition
"The Lord reigns. He is robed in majesty. Let us shout aloud to the Rock of our salvation! Bless the Lord, O my soul and all that is within me bless His holy name. O give thanks to the Lord for He is good. For His loving kindness is everlasting. Let the redeemed of the Lord say so!" [from Psalms 93, 95, 103, 107] There it is . . . right in His Word. If we believe in Him, we need to say so!

I Believe in Jesus (2 times through—slow, then faster)

Transition
We so often sanitize the actual death of Christ on the cross. We don't think about His hands tearing and

bleeding as the nails ripped into them. We don't think about His nailed-together feet supporting the weight of His body. We don't think about the spear piercing and entering His side or the thorns crushing into His forehead. We don't think about the agony He experienced just to take a shallow breath to continue to live. We often don't think about the fact that He was also God and could have stopped it all; but His Father had said this was the way—and Christ obeyed. As we worship the Lord, think about His humanity. Think about our need that only the suffering of His humanity can meet.

You Are My All in All (solos on vv.; all on choruses with keys ascending each time)
   Beneath the Cross of Jesus (v. 2: solo)
   Rock of Ages (all, 1 time—in 4/4)
   We Will Worship (slow and fast; end slow)

MESSAGE
   "I Thirst" [see chap. 9, Sermon 4]

THE LORD'S SUPPER
The Bread
   O Sacred Head Now Wounded (SATB quartet: v. 1 SATB
      a cappella; v. 2 unison with keyboard)
   Draw Me Nearer (all: 2 times, chorus only)
   Jesus, Draw Me Close (all: 1 time; solo: 1 time in Spanish;
      all: 1 time in higher key)

The Cup
   Band:
      Think About His Love

Jesus Paid It All
Oh, How He Loves You and Me

INVITATION
Take Up Your Cross

BENEVOLENCE OFFERING
Piano: *How Excellent*

CLOSING SONG
Lord, I Lift Your Name

POSTSERVICE
(Live band or CD/cassette)

Contributed by David Taylor
First Baptist Church, Orlando, Florida

Service 8:
General

PRELUDE

CHORUS
Blessed Be the Lord, God Almighty (2-line solo; all: 2 times)

INVOCATION

SPECIAL MUSIC
Were You There?

WELCOME

MEDLEY ON THE CROSS
At the Cross (vv. 1, 4)
Near the Cross (v. 1)
The Old Rugged Cross (v. 1)
At the Cross (refrain only)
O How He Loves You and Me (chorus: 1 time)

OFFERTORY PRAYER

OFFERTORY
Embrace the Cross

SCRIPTURE
Romans 5:6–11

MEDITATION
"The Cross: It Took Just One—Once" [see chap. 9, Sermon 10]

LORD'S SUPPER
Bread
Handbell Choir
  Near The Cross
  Fill My Cup, Lord

Cup:
Congregational Singing
  Nothing but the Blood (v. 1 in E-flat)
  O the Blood of Jesus (1 time in E-flat; 1 time in F)
  When I Survey the Wondrous Cross (v. 1 in F)
  There's Pow'r in the Blood (v. 1 with chorus in B-flat; chorus only in C)

INVITATION
  'Tis So Sweet to Trust in Jesus

CLOSING REMARKS

CLOSING CHORUS
  In My Life, Lord (1 time in C; 1 time in D)

POSTLUDE

**Contributed by worship team
First Baptist Church, Orlando, Florida**

Service 9:
General

PRELUDE
  Orchestra: *There Is a Savior*

BAPTISM

CHORUS
  Family of God (chorus: 1 time)

INVOCATION

HYMN/CHORUS MEDLEY
  Standing on the Promises (vv. 1, 2, 4)
  Come into His Presence (1 time)
  How Great Thou Art (refrain only)

WELCOME

PARENT AND BABY DEDICATION

PRAISE PACKAGE
  Alas! And Did My Savior Bleed (vv. 1, 4)
  There's Just Something about That Name (1 time)
  I Sing Praises to Your Name, O Lord (1 time)
  Glory to Your Name (refrain only)

OFFERTORY PRAYER

OFFERTORY
  Choir: *All the Way My Savior Leads Me*

MESSAGE

"Abusing and Misusing the Lord's Supper" 1 Corinthians 11:17–34 [see chap. 9, Sermon 5]

LORD'S SUPPER

Bread

Orchestra: *Beneath the Cross of Jesus*
When I Survey the Wondrous Cross

Cup

Choir and congregation sing a cappella:
Old Rugged Cross (v. 1 and refrain)
Praise Your Name, Lord Jesus (1 time)
My Jesus, I Love Thee (v. 1)
Lead Me to Calvary (v. 1 and refrain)
At Calvary (refrain only)

INVITATION
Just As I Am

BENEVOLENCE OFFERTORY
Instrumental: *In the Name of the Lord*

CLOSING REMARKS

CLOSING SONG
Holy, Holy

POSTLUDE

Contributed by worship team
First Baptist Church, Orlando, Florida

Service 10:
General

PRELUDE
> Instrumental: *Were You There/The Old Rugged Cross*
> Vocal Soloist: *The Old Rugged Cross*

SCRIPTURE
> Mark 15:33–39

[The worship leader comments on how the cross of Christ obviously made a difference to a man, the centurion, who did not even follow Christ and extends an invitation for those who follow Christ to remember and celebrate the Lord's Supper.]

CONGREGATIONAL WORSHIP
> *Amazing Grace* (2 verses in G)
> *Grace Greater Than All Our Sin* (refrain plus 1 verse in G)
> *Lord, I Lift Your Name on High* (1 time in G)
> *Under the Blood* (1 time in G)

MESSAGE
> "The Most Meaningful Memorial in the World" [see chap. 9, Sermon 6]

DISTRIBUTION OF THE BREAD
> *Were You There* (vv. 1, 2 in E flat)
> *There's Something about That Name* (1 time in E-flat)

[The congregation sings while the bread is being distributed. Worship leader prays for the bread, followed by the congregation's eating of the bread.]

DISTRIBUTION OF THE CUP
Nothing but the Blood (v. 1 in G)
Whiter Than Snow (v. 3 in G)
Under the Blood (refrain only in G)
[The congregation sings while the cup is being distributed. Worship leader prays for the cup, followed by the congregation's drinking of the cup.]

CONGREGATIONAL WORSHIP
Because He Lives (refrain only in G)
In Christ Alone (1 time in G; 1 time in A-flat)
Shine, Jesus, Shine (chorus only: 2 times in G)

Contributed by Bob Russell
Southeast Christian Church, Louisville, Kentucky

Service 11:
General

ORGAN PRELUDE

ANNOUNCEMENTS

PRAYER CHORUS (Choir)

CALL TO PRAYER

SOLO (Vocal)

WELCOME AND FELLOWSHIP

WELCOME CHORUS
O How He Loves You and Me

MISSION MOMENTS/OFFERTORY PRAYER

OFFERTORY
Choir: *They Could Not*

THE LORD'S SUPPER

Introduction of Lord's Supper
"This Do Ye" (1 Cor. 11:23–26) [see chap. 9, Sermon 7]

The Supper Is a Remembrance of the Past
Hymn: *The Old Rugged Cross*

The Supper Is a Time of Unity and Fellowship of the Present
Hymn: *Sweet, Sweet Spirit*

The Supper Is an Anticipation of the Future
Hymn: *Face to Face with Christ, My Savior*

The Supper Is a Time of Invitation
Hymn: *When I Survey the Wondrous Cross*

The Serving of the Bread
Choir: *Shalom*

The Serving of the Cup
Choir: *In Remembrance of Me*

RECEIVING OF NEW MEMBERS

CLOSING HYMN
Blest Be the Tie That Binds

Contributed by Roy T. Edgemon
Director, Discipleship and Family Development
Division, Baptist Sunday School Board, Nashville, Tennessee

Service 12:
General

PRELUDE
   Orchestra: *Are You Washed in the Blood*

BAPTISM/PRAYER

CONGREGATIONAL PRAISE
   At Calvary (vv. 1, 2, 4)
   Jesus, Your Name (all vv.)

SPECIAL MUSIC
   Men's Quartet: *Shine on Us*

WELCOME/FELLOWSHIP HYMN
   I Will Serve Thee (all vv.)

PRAYER/OFFERTORY
   Choir and Orchestra: *Written in Red*

MESSAGE
   "This Do Remembering Him" [see chap. 9, Sermon 9]

THE LORD'S SUPPER
   Bread
      Choral Ensemble: *The Communion Song*
   Cup
      Choral Ensemble: *We Remember You*

INVITATION
   Lead Me, Lord
   Jesus, Your Name

DECISIONS/CLOSING REMARKS

POSTLUDE
   Orchestra: *God's Amazing Grace*

   Contributed by Johnny M. Hunt
   First Baptist Church, Woodstock, Georgia

Service 13:
Contemporary/General

PRESERVICE MUSIC
[Live band or instrumental CD/cassette]

WORSHIP PACKAGE
Hallelujah, Jesus Is Alive (2 times through all)
Celebrate Jesus (2 times through all)

Transition
People all over the world celebrate dead gods, but we celebrate a living and personal God! What did the angel say to the women at the tomb of Jesus Christ? "Why do you seek the living among the dead? He is not here, for He is risen!"

Hallelujah, Jesus Is Alive (1 time through with big ending)

Transition
We couldn't celebrate if Christ hadn't paid the price on the cross. Take a few minutes to dwell on the importance of the Cross in your life.

At the Cross (1 time solo on v./chorus; all: 2 times on chorus only—up-tempo with R&B feel)
O, the Blood of Jesus (all: 2 times: black gospel feel, modulating into 2nd time)
The Blood Will Never Lose Its Power (solo)

Transition

Have you experienced a change in your life that only the blood of Christ can bring? Have you experienced the power?

At Calvary (solo on v.; all: 2 times on chorus—ballad feel)

By Your Blood (all: 2 times on chorus—up-tempo, modulating 2nd time)

Nothing but the Blood (vv. 1, 2: solo on vv. with all responding; all on chorus; all: vv. 3, 4—modulate on both, growing grander each time)

MESSAGE

"The Precious Blood of Christ" [see chap. 9, Sermon 11]

THE LORD'S SUPPER

The Bread

[The following package is instrumental, preferably solo instrument (e.g., soprano sax) with rhythm section backup. A keyboard with rhythm section backup if solo instrument not possible.]

A Perfect Heart

There Is a Redeemer

My Tribute

The Cup

[Vocal package sung with band backup:]

Touch of Grace (solo on vv.; all on choruses)

Amazing Grace (all on vv. 1, 2, in 4/4)

Grace Greater than Our Sin (all: 1 time on chorus)

Touch of Grace (all on chorus)

INVITATION
Change My Heart, O God

BENEVOLENCE OFFERING
Band: *The Strong Name of Jesus*

CLOSING SONG
The Strong Name of Jesus (chorus only)

POSTSERVICE
[Band or instrumental CD/cassette]

Contributed by David Taylor
First Baptist Church, Orlando, Florida

Service 14:
General/Christmas/Lenten/Drama

NOTE: The following is not a complete order of worship. It is a dramatic presentation to be performed by a couple (dressed in street clothing) during the serving of the elements.

[The first element, the bread, is beginning to be served. After a moment, a man and a woman enter, approaching the platform/pulpit area. As they reach their position, the man turns 3/4 back to the audience. The woman stops and immediately begins to speak directly to the audience.]

Woman I remember those tiny hands. They were the very first thing I noticed. *[She positions her arms and hands as to cradle a newborn baby.]* As this new little earth visitor cried, He stretched those hands from under the covers. I couldn't resist placing my finger in the path, so that one of His hands would encounter it. And . . . when it happened . . . when, for the first time we touched and He grasped His mother's finger, I knew my life was changed . . . forever. *[She freezes in position, looking down at the "baby in her arms." At the same moment, the man turns and moves past her, still in close proximity to her position. As he turns, he speaks facing off right center. The flow of their speaking never breaks.]*

Man Soon that little fellow began to run and play and laugh and speak. Now, I saw those same hands growing, exploring, learning, strengthening for His work. And when He touched my big arm or reached up to me to embrace Him . . . no one could resist his love. *[He remains motionless, staring straight ahead, to left center. The woman speaks immediately.]*

Woman: As He grew into manhood, His love grew. And, those same hands . . . now . . . straightened the arm of the crippled, touched the eyes of the blind, and reached into the very soul to replace the hurt with healing.

Man And . . . His embrace! In that big embrace, the world found retreat, safety, acceptance . . . love.

Woman Later that embrace was pulled apart. To put an end to His touch.

Man But, in those parting arms, His embrace *[as he speaks his own arms are pulled by unseen forces stretching side to side, the width of his reach]* was stretched to its full extent! *[His arms are stretched as if on a cross.]* He could reach no further than when they nailed Him to that cross. *[He remains in that position and lowers his head.]*

Woman *[Quickly.]* See from His head, His hands, His feet. Sorrow and . . . love . . . flow mingled down. *[Her actions follow her words until she is kneeling at "the foot of the cross."]*

Man *[The man slowly lowers his hands.]* But . . . the story isn't over yet.

[They move to a place convenient for remaining on the platform, out of the flow of the service.]

[The second element of the Lord's Supper, the cup, is beginning to be served. After a moment, the man and the woman move toward downstage to their positions. They speak with great emotion and energy! There is no break between their lines.]

Man When I survey His wondrous cross . . .

Woman On which the Prince of Glory died . . . my richest gain I count but loss!

Man And pour contempt on all my pride. *[The man slowly resumes the cross stance as previously played.]*

Woman See . . . from His head, His hands, His feet! Sorrow and love flow mingled down. Did e'er such love and sorrow meet . . . or thorns compose *[Sudden stop— staccato]* so . . . rich . . . a . . . crown?

[The man lowers his arms and again becomes a part of the presentation of the spoken word.]

Woman *[Spoken so that the meaning is abundantly clear.]* Were the whole realm of nature mine . . . that is a present far too small . . . *[No break . . . directly into . . .]*

Man LOVE! So amazing, so divine . . . demands *[break]* my soul, *[break]* my life, *[break]* my all.

Woman But the story isn't over yet.

Man The blood was not loss. It was love.

Woman Love was not defeated. It was VICTORIOUS!

Contributed by R. Wayne Johnson
First Baptist Church, Orlando, Florida

Service 15:
Lenten/Maundy Thursday

PRELUDE
Jesus Comforts the Women of Jerusalem (Dupré)

CALL TO WORSHIP
Minister
Jesus said: "Go and make preparations for us to eat the Passover" (Luke 22:8). In remembrance of that occasion, we have come together tonight to share the cup and the loaf, and to know the power of the new covenant.

HYMN
Let Us Break Bread Together

PRAYER
Minister and People
Our Father, we are thankful that we can count upon Your presence as we come together to celebrate Christ's love for us. As Christ was with His friends in the upper room, we give thanks that His presence is also with us here tonight. May our hearts be open to the reality of Christ's presence, so that the power and inspiration of this service will go beyond these moments to change all of life for us. May we truly feel that Christ is sharing these elements of bread and wine with us, and may we be worthy guests at His table. In Christ's name, Amen.

HYMN
There Is a Fountain

ANTHEM

God So Loved the World (Stainer)

LITANY

Minister: Jesus and His friends gathered in an upper room for a fellowship meal.

People: We have gathered here for a fellowship meal with family, friends, and the Spirit of Christ.

Minister: The meal was a time to remember God's deliverance in the Exodus.

People: We come together to remember what Christ's giving Himself has done for us.

Minister: It was also a time for the disciples to examine their motives and actions to question if betrayal would come from them.

People: May this be a time when each of us shall closely examine our attitude towards Christ to see if betrayal—word or deed—has been our sin.

Minister: Jesus told His disciples of a new agreement that would be instituted between God and His people.

People: May we live in the knowledge of this new covenant that gives us the opportunity for a deeper understanding of God's love for us and of His desire to forgive and redeem us.

Minister: After supper, Jesus girded Himself with a towel and washed His disciples' feet.

People: We accept the fact that we express our love for Jesus as we love and serve others.

Minister: Jesus said, "Do this in remembrance of me."

People: In remembrance of Him—His life, death and resurrection—we commit ourselves anew to Him, His work and His gospel. Amen.

PASTORAL PRAYER

SOLO
O Divine Redeemer (Gounod)

MEDITATION
"The Upper Room: A Time to Remember" [see chap. 9, Sermon 12]

LORD'S SUPPER

HYMN

BENEDICTION

POSTLUDE
Jesus, Our Lord, We Adore Thee (Dubois)

Contributed by Charles A. Graves
United Methodist minister, Spartanburg, South Carolina

Service 16:
Labor Day/General

WELCOME/CHURCH NEWS

GREETING
My Life Is in You, Lord

SCRIPTURE/PRAYER/BAPTISM
In My Life, Lord, Be Glorified

CHORUS OF PRAISE
The Name of the Lord

HYMNS
His Name Is Wonderful
My Jesus, I Love You

CHORUS OF PRAISE
White as Snow

PRAISE
Vocal Duet: *Worthy Is the Lamb*

THE LORD'S SUPPER
"The Power of Spiritual Memory" [see chap. 9, Sermon 13]

TIME OF INVITATION
Lead Me, Lord

PRAYER/OFFERING/INSTRUMENTAL PRAISE

BENEDICTION CHORUS
  No Other Name

Contributed by David H. McKinley
First Baptist Church, Merritt Island, Florida

Service 17:
World Communion Sunday

WORD OF WELCOME

PRELUDE
"Spiritoso," *Organ Concerto No. 9* (Handel)

INTROIT
Sweet, Sweet Spirit

TIME FOR SINGING
Seek Ye First
His Name Is Wonderful
Surely the Presence

PRAYER

TIME FOR YOUNG DISCIPLES
Communion around the World

PRAYER FOR THE NATION
America (Congregational Hymn)

OFFERTORY PRAYER

OFFERTORY
Come to the Table of the Lord (Albrechr/Althouse)

SCRIPTURE
Matthew 26:26–29

SERMON
   "The Whole World in His Hands"

DOXOLOGY

THE LORD'S SUPPER

   [The congregation and choir will sing *Alleluia* through
   once and then hum its tune during the invitation, words of
   institution, and prayer.]

Invitation to Share

Words of Institution

Prayer of Celebration

Sharing the Loaf and the Cup
   Male Solo: *Embrace the Cross* (Wolaver/Linn)
   Choir: *Agnus Dei* (Fauré)
   Organ: "Adagio," *7th Symphony* (Bruckner)
   Choir/Solo/Congregation/Organ/Flute: *Jesus, Remember
Me*   (Berthier)

PRAYER OF THANKSGIVING

HYMN
   The Lord's Prayer (Mallotte)

RECOGNITION OF NEW MEMBERS

INVITATION TO CHRISTIAN DISCIPLESHIP

CLOSING PRAYER

CHORAL BENEDICTION
   Grace Be with You (Taylor)

POSTLUDE
   Our Father in Heaven (Schneider)

Contributed by Howard Edington
First Presbyterian Church, Orlando, Florida

Service 18:
Thanksgiving

WELCOME/CHURCH NEWS

GREETING
I Will Sing of the Mercies

SCRIPTURE/PRAYER/BAPTISM
In My Life, Lord, Be Glorified

PRAISE MEDLEY
The Name of the Lord
Thou Art Worthy, Great Jehovah
Come, Ye Thankful People, Come

SEASON OF PRAYER AND THANKSGIVING

CHORUS OF PRAISE
Give Thanks

PRAISE
Vocal Solo: *My Tribute*

THE LORD'S SUPPER
"Come to the Table" 1 Cor. 11:23–29 [see chap. 9, Sermon 14]

TIME OF INVITATION
Lead Me, Lord

PRAYER/OFFERTORY (Instrumental)

NEW MEMBER PRESENTATION
   Thank You, Lord, for Saving My Soul

BENEDICTION CHORUS
   Doxology

   Contributed by David H. McKinley
   First Baptist Church, Merritt Island, Florida

Service 19:
Advent/Christmas

PRELUDE

INVOCATION

CONGREGATIONAL HYMN
O Little Town of Bethlehem

CHRISTMAS RESPONSIVE READING

CONGREGATIONAL RESPONSE
O Come Let Us Adore Him (refrain only)

SPECIAL MUSIC
O Holy Night

CHRISTMAS PRAYER

COMMUNION MESSAGE
"A Christmas Communion" [see chap. 9, Sermon 15]

CHRISTMAS SCRIPTURE
Luke 2:1–20

[While the Scripture is being read, actors portraying Mary, Joseph, shepherds, and angels take their places around the manger in which the communion elements are placed. Background music should be played during the reading of the Scripture.]

COMMUNION INVITATION

[At this point in the service, explain the *symbolism* of the elements in the manger and the method of serving the congregation. You may include any ritual appropriate to your church's tradition.]

SERVING OF THE ELEMENTS

[The elements are placed in the crèche of the manger scene. While quiet music is being played, pastors move to the manger and lift each element as it is to be served. First, a loaf wrapped in swaddling cloth is lifted and cradled like a baby—to symbolize the body of the Christ child. (As the pastors are served, they should gently break the loaf and eat.) Next, a chalice is lifted from the manger (symbolizing Christ's blood) and treated in a similar fashion. During this time, appropriate words of inspiration and explanation should be given.]

CONCLUDING RITUAL

[This should be done as is normal to your church's tradition.]

HYMN OF CELEBRATION

Joy to the World [conclude with congregational candle lighting]

BENEDICTION

Contributed by William A. Pickett
Pine Castle United Methodist Church, Orlando, Florida

Service 20:
Contemporary/Christmas

PRESERVICE MUSIC
[Live band or instrumental CD/cassette of updated version of Christmas carol (e.g., jazz, reggae, etc.)]

WORSHIP PACKAGE
Keyboard under spoken intro
While Mary and Joseph were in Bethlehem to pay their taxes, she gave birth to Jesus. And the angels praised God, singing, "Glory to God in the highest!"

Angels We Have Heard on High (chorus only 2 times, modulate into 2nd time)
Joy to the World (v. 1: all)
O Come, Let Us Adore Him (3 times with keys ascending each time)
1. O Come, let us adore Him . . .
2. We'll praise Your name forever . . .
3. For You alone are worthy . . .
Isn't He (congregation echoes worship leader)

Transition
Our understanding—of how beautiful and wonderful Christ is—is limited to our finite human minds and earthly comparisons of beauty. His sacrifice for each of us on the cross, however, should give us just a little heavenly understanding of the depth of His beauty expressed in His love gift of drops of blood.

Think about His Love (2 or 3 times)
Yes, Jesus Loves Me (chorus only 2 times)

Transition
Worship the Lord of love now for who He is.

I Worship You, Almighty God (2 times with last line tagged several times on final time)

MESSAGE
"Finding the Perfect Gift"

THE LORD'S SUPPER

[The following packages for the elements are single verses of Christmas carols that deal with the blood and sacrifice of Christ. They should be sung as solos and tied together instrumentally. If additional time is needed, each hymn verse could be introduced with a one- time run-through by the keyboard or band.]

The Bread
Come, Thou Long-Expected Jesus (v. 2 beginning "Born . . .")
O Holy Night (v. 2 beginning "With . . .")
While by Our Sheep (v. 3 beginning "There shall the Child . . .")
What Child Is This? (v. 3 beginning "So . . .")

The Cup
O Little Town of Bethlehem (v. 4 beginning "O holy . . .")
O Come, O Come, Emmanuel (v. 2 beginning "O come, Thou rod . . .")
Thou Didst Leave Thy Throne (v. 4 beginning "Thou . . .")

The First Noel (v. 6 beginning "Now let . . .")

INVITATION
Emmanuel

BENEVOLENCE OFFERING
Band: *Go, Tell It on the Mountain* (Band)

CLOSING SONG
Go, Tell It on the Mountain (jazz style)

POSTSERVICE
(Live band or CD/cassette)

Contributed by David Taylor
First Baptist Church, Orlando, Florida

Service Ideas:
Lord's Supper Worship Features

Following is a list of ideas that incorporate dramatic visual ministry that may be used to enhance the observance of the Lord's Supper.

1. This feature must be done with great discretion: As the first element is being served, have a man dressed as Christ enter the room. This will work best if the entrance is from the rear of the room. The individual portraying Christ must be carefully chosen for a number of reasons—spiritual ones paramount. Physical appearance must be well-prepared, as well. The person wanders through the room, pausing here and there to look about the room, to exchange a glance with a worshiper, to kneel at the pulpit area, or just to move slowly through the room, stopping as he feels led. No contact is made with any one person. He finally selects an exit that is visible to all.

This may be done with soft music playing (vocal not suggested.) For greatest effect, have no sound in the room. As soon as Christ exits, the pastor leads the congregation to take the element.

2. A wide range of video is available today for use in a Lord's Supper service. Clips from films may be used if copyright clearance is secured. Check with Christian bookstores and/or film services.

3. The use of tableaux is a simple and inexpensive feature. In an isolated spot in the worship center, where basic lighting can be utilized, small intimate scenes—biblical or modern—

can be set up and highlighted for emphasis during the service. Costuming can be as simple or as elaborate as you desire.

4. For a Lord's Supper celebration with a missions emphasis, have individuals dressed in national costumes. Just before or as the service begins, they enter the room and sit in various places—not all together. They sit alone, partake of the Lord's Supper and, perhaps as the service is closed, the pastor calls them forward. The pastor reminds the congregation that this observance is celebrated around the world by fellow believers who are supported by our gifts. This same idea could also be used with the entry of a homeless family who enters and partakes of the Supper. Several applications could be made by the pastor following the close of the service.

5. Some churches utilize choreographed movement to selected hymns that match the Supper celebration. If this is done it should be done tastefully and with professional guidance. If your church has not used choreography in worship, it would probably be best to introduce it in other settings before using it at the Lord's Supper.

Contributed by R. Wayne Johnson
First Baptist Church, Orlando, Florida

CHAPTER NINE

The Proclamation

❖

The symbolism of the Lord's Supper carries an inherent dynamic that speaks for itself. In addition, the Supper is for Christians one of those "teachable moments," just as Passover has been for the Hebrew community for more than four thousand years. The following are message outlines you can use preceding, during, or following the Lord's Supper observance. You may also choose to use a vignette, an illustration, a dramatic presentation, Scripture passages, or a video instead of a full message. I have used all of these approaches to the Lord's Table through the years and have found them all effective.

Sermon 1:
General

TITLE: **"The Perfect Life Together: Serving the Poor, the Outcast"**

SCRIPTURE: Matthew 20:25–34; 2 Corinthians 8:9

In the life of service together as God's church, we are called to do whatever individual acts of service are presented to us daily. Yet, I believe the church must be especially caring as we serve others in this culture. We live in a time when there is growing disparity between the rich and the poor. As a result, people look more and more to the government for compassion. What has happened to the church?

I. The Hijacking of the Church (Matt. 20:25–34)

The church has somehow gotten hijacked from its original compassion for *those who have not.* We have begun to equate spirituality with personal growth. While personal growth is essential, we leave out a very substantial—and critical—part of the job of the church. It is essential because it was a part of who Christ was, and the church is supposed to reflect the image of Christ.

A. The Compassionate Church (Acts 2:44–47)

In New Testament times, Christians were the ones who cared for others. They not only took care of other Christians, but they also took care of the orphans. They stood against infanticide. They were the ones who took into their fold the wounded and the outcast, whether or not these were Christians.

B. The Consumer Church (Rom. 1:20–23; 1 John 3:17–18)

The church has moved forward and been successful over the centuries. It's been so successful that it did not have to pay attention to those who were outcast, wounded, and hurting. It had enough, so the church could continue doing as it had done for many years. We live in a consumer-oriented society. That's what our capitalism and our mass media do—they build consumers. The church has become selfish.

II. God's Resource for the Poor (2 Cor. 8:9)

A. God's Targeted Audience (Luke 4:18–19, 6:20–26)

Notice God's targeted audience as listed in Luke 4:18–19. It's not just the monetarily poor; it's those who are captive. It's those who are blind and those who are downtrodden. As the church incorporates those who are without, it is incorporating those whom Christ loved—and those whom He calls us to love.

B. God's Targeted Tool (2 Cor. 8:13–15)

It is the church's special responsibility, if we've been blessed, to supply the needs of the downtrodden. Very early in church history—when the church was going through one of its times of persecution—it was rumored in the Roman Empire that the church was hoarding all kinds of wealth. It was furthered rumored that the church had storehouses of gold. (This was before the church had any wealth at all.)

So the authorities called in the Bishop Lawrence. They said to him, "We want the church to turn over to us the treasures of the church." Lawrence answered, "We have no treasures." He did not convince the authorities who continued to insist, "We know you do! We will come to your church tomorrow, and you *will* give us your treasure!"

The following day they showed up at the bishop's church. As they entered the church, they saw the poor, the blind, the sick, and the orphaned. Bishop Lawrence looked up at the authorities and said, "Truthfully, *these* are the treasures of the church."

III. God's Forgiveness of Debt, and Ours (Matt. 26:28)

A. The Jubilee Principle (Lev. 25:9–24)

In Leviticus 25, we read of the year of Jubilee that was observed by God's chosen people every fiftieth year. Resources were returned to those who had lost them. That is, if a family had lost their land because of sickness or economic problems, the land was returned to them in the year of Jubilee. I believe God wanted them—and us—to understand that all resources belong to Him alone. We own no resources. All that we have—all that is in our possession—is only the productivity of His resources, which He has entrusted to our care. The Jubilee principle is the principle that we, as God's people, should give back to others what they need in order to be productive. Our assistance could help enable people to break the cycle of poverty (whether it be monetary, emotional, or spiritual).

B. The Banquet Principle (Luke 14:12–14)

In Luke 14, Jesus gives us instructions about whom should be fed: those who cannot pay us back. The verb tense in Greek indicates that it is an ongoing responsibility, and the mood indicates that it is an order! The banquet principle is one of the most beloved principles because it is most like our relationship to God. *We* were the poor, the crippled, the blind. He gave to us when we could not repay or even fully appreciate what He had done for us.

My grandfather used to laugh at an incident that happened to him during the depression. My grandparents lived along the railroad tracks and got a steady stream of hobos looking for handouts. They always managed to find something for them to eat. One day a man came but kept looking at my father while he ate. When the hobo finished, he said, "No offense, sir, but you're about the homeliest man I've ever seen!" Pop laughed as he recounted those special memories. It impressed me how he always drew great joy from being able to give to those who could not repay. So does God. So should we.

Contributed by Joel Hunter
Northland Community Church, Longwood, Florida

Sermon 2:
General

TITLE: **"Behold, the Lamb of God!"**

SCRIPTURE: Mark 15:33–40

During the Great Depression, a Missouri man named Don Griffith controlled the railroad drawbridge across the Mississippi River. In the summer of 1937, he took his eight-year-old son, Greg, to work with him. At noon, he put the bridge up to allow ships their passage. Enjoying the presence of his son, he lost track of time. At 1:07, he was startled by the *Memphis Express* blowing its whistle in the distance. He dashed to the controls and prepared to lower the bridge.

Just before releasing the master lever, he panicked as he caught sight of his son. His son had slipped from the observation deck, and now he had his leg caught in the cogs of the main gears. Griffith quickly thought of a plan to rescue his boy, but there was no time. The express train carrying four hundred passengers was bearing down on the bridge. Saving his son would cost the lives of the passengers.

In anguish, Don Griffith threw the lever and watched his son die in the cogs of the gears. His son's death spared the lives of all the passengers on the train. As they sped by, great heartache followed as a numb Griffith stared into the windows of the speeding train. He saw passengers reading their newspapers and sipping coffee in the dining car—oblivious to the price that had been paid to save their lives. No one even looked his way to acknowledge his great sacrifice and overwhelming grief. Through tear-stained eyes, he screamed at the top of his voice to the passing train, "I sacrificed my son for you people! Don't you even care?"

Sacrificial love costs. Sacrificial love gives—and keeps giving.

I. Behold, the Lamb!

Mary stood and watched, in disbelief and anguish, as her Son was slaughtered like a lamb. His death had been foretold by the prophet Isaiah: "He was led like a lamb to the slaughter, and as a sheep before her shearers is silent, so he did not open his mouth" (Isa. 53:7). The scene of her son hanging on the cross like a slaughtered lamb brought back to her memory the haunting words of John the Baptist. When John saw Jesus approaching the Jordan River that day, he cried, "Look, the Lamb of God, who takes away the sin of the world!" (John 1:29).

II. Characteristics of the Lamb

There are numerous characteristics of a lamb. Mary struggled to see these reflected in her Son:

- Lambs wander aimlessly, but Jesus had always been purposely focused.

- Lambs need constant care, but Jesus had always consistently given care.

- Lambs are slow to respond, but Jesus had always quickly responded to those in need.

To Mary, it seemed like He had been much more like a shepherd than a lamb.

III. Importance of the Lamb

It seemed that for Mary's lamb there was but one ominous meaning, one ultimate purpose: *sacrifice.*

Mary's mind raced back to the night when shepherds, summoned by the angel's announcement, had come to the manger. These men had been tending sheep that were to be slaughtered sacrificially at the temple. This event seemed to reinforce the meaning of her Son's being the precious Lamb of God, born to die to cover man's sin.

Mary also remembered watching as her Son, sitting at Joseph's knee, heard stories of the lamb throughout the redemptive history of God:

- Abel had sacrificed a lamb. It was a *sacrifice for an individual.*

- Lambs were slaughtered on the night of the Exodus. These were *sacrifices for families.*

- On the day of atonement, a lamb was sacrificed. It was a *sacrifice for the whole nation.*

Now, as Mary stood before the cross, her Lamb was being sacrificed. He was a *sacrifice for the world.*

IV. Cost for the Lamb

As Mary stood listening to the crowds around her, she heard the religious leaders yell, *"It is over!"*

As the disciples began to walk away from the cross, Mary heard the disciples express, *"We're through!"*

And then Mary heard the cry of her Son from the cross: *"It is finished!"*

Let us all be reminded of the agony endured by this spotless Lamb and the supreme cost for our salvation.

[At this point, show the video portion of the crucifixion from the *Jesus of Nazareth* movie. When the film segment has been shown, the pastor should immediately dismiss the people to go to the fellowship hall and should direct them to go in silence.]

[The fellowship hall should be filled with tables set with pitchers of grape juice and platters of unleavened bread. A deacon should stand at each table. As people enter the fellowship hall, they should be instructed to go to the tables by household units and be seated. Once seated, begin by allowing the head of each household to pray aloud for each family member of household. If there are those without family members present at the table, have the deacon pray for them or have them pray for each other. At the direction of the pastor, partake of the elements. When the Lord's Supper has been served, each table should sing a hymn and depart.]

[NOTE: If the fellowship hall is too small to handle the entire congregation, the congregation can be split. While half of the congregation begins with the Lord's Supper in the fellowship hall, the other half can be worshiping in the sanctuary. When finished, they exchange locations.]

Contributed by Robert E. Reccord
National Mission Board of the Southern Baptist Convention

Sermon 3:
General

TITLE: **"Universal Magnetism"** [see chap. 8, Service 6]

SCRIPTURE: John 12:32–33

The Lord's Supper is a memorial to the *incarnate life* and the *sacrificial death* of Christ. Let us examine three truths about the Cross from this passage in John.

I. The Magnetic Person on the Cross

- "I, when I. . . to myself" (v. 32).

- The Christ of the Cross.

A. The world has always had men and women of charismatic, magnetic, and commanding personality (for example, Napoleon and Churchill).

B. Jesus Christ is the most magnetic person who ever lived—then and now.

John records seven great "I Am's" by Jesus: *Bread,* 6:35; *Light,* 8:12; *Door,* 10:7; *Good Shepherd,* 10:11; *Resurrection and Life,* 11:25; *Way, Truth, and Life,* 14:6; *Vine,* 15:1.

C. Who was on the cross is what makes the difference.

Jesus had ordinary men hanging on each side of him. He was not just a man, martyr, prophet, or teacher; He was the God-Man, the sinless One—God (John 1:1, 14; 1 Pet. 2:22).

II. The Magnetic Passion of the Cross

- "Lifted up from the earth" (v. 32).

- The Christ *on* the cross.

- We move from His person to His passion, and from His character to His cross.

A. Luke used the term passion or suffering to refer to the last week of Christ's life (Acts 1:3).

B. Jesus used the words lifted up three times—each time describing a different purpose in the Passion:

1. *The reason for the Cross* (John 3:14–15). There can be no forgiveness of sins without the cross. There can be no pardon, no hope, no peace.

2. *The revelation of the Cross* (John 8:28). Jesus was revealing God to man.

3. *The reign of the Cross* (John 12:31, 32). Satan was and ultimately will be defeated by the Cross.

III. The Magnetic Power in the Cross

- "Will draw all men" (v. 32).

- Christ seen through the cross.

A. Christ draws men.

B. Christ draws all men.

C. Christ draws all men unto himself.

Conclusion

As we draw near to the Lord's Table, let us draw near to the One who offered up Himself on the cross to victoriously accomplish that which the Father ordained: the redemption of those who are drawn, in faith, to Christ.

Lifted up was He to die,
"It is finished!" was His cry;
Now in heaven exalted high:
Hallelujah! What a Savior![4]

Contributed by James M. Knott
First Baptist Church, Orlando, Florida

Sermon 4:
General/Lenten

TITLE: **"I Thirst"** [see chap. 8, Service 7]

SCRIPTURE: John 19:28–30

The word *dipso* has only four letters in Greek. It was spoken by Christ from the cross. It is the briefest utterance of Jesus' "seven last words." David James Burrell says, "It is as brief as the wail of a little child." Charles Spurgeon describes this word of our Lord as "short, but [I] cannot say sweet . . . but out of bitterness I trust there will come great sweetness to us."

The sun was beginning to shine again. It was shortly after 3:00 P.M. Jesus had been on the cross for six hours. It had grown quiet. The howling mob had been silenced by the sun's hiding its face from the horror unleashed against its Creator. Jesus, weakened by His suffering, cried out, "I am thirsty!"

This word is different from the other words spoken by our Lord from the cross. It is not a request made out of concern for souls or words reflecting the forsakenness of the Son of God or the parting cry of a laborer laying down his task. Rather, this word reflects the human Christ, calling attention to Himself.

Christ was offered three cups at Calvary:

1. *The Opiate:* Jesus refused the first cup (Matt. 27:34). He wanted clarity and clearness of thought in these last moments.

2. *The Mockery:* Jesus refused this second cup of mockery (Luke 23:36).

3. The Refreshing Drink: Jesus, fully God, fully man, received the refreshing drink that ministered to His human condition (John 19:28–30).

This Word from the Cross impacts our faith venture in at least five important ways:

I. Incarnation

Jesus Christ, the Lord of the universe, loved us so much that He took on the form of a human infant, born of a woman into a meager station in life. He became God-Man, not two separate personalities, but one perfect Being who possessed two distinct natures.

As we take the cup at His Table, let us remember our Lord's word of humanity from the cross, "I am thirsty." Our Savior chose to identify Himself perfectly with all our human needs. He took on the frailty of our human nature, so He could face any challenge we might face—even a horrible death.

II. Intensity of His Suffering

Of course, Jesus had known thirst before. When He was passing through Samaria, He stopped at Jacob's well and asked a woman, "Will you give me a drink?" (John 4:7). While on the cross, however, Jesus experienced the most acute thirst of His life. It had been quite some time since His last drink—perhaps the final sip at the Last Supper, eighteen hours earlier. Since then, He had undergone tremendous physiological trauma, the sweating of drops of blood at Gethsemane, the mockery of interrogation and trial, being dragged from one place in the city to another, the lashing with the Roman cat-o'-nine-tails, the scorn of the crowds and the soldiers, the crown of thorns, and the laborious *Via Dolorosa*.

Naked on the cross, Jesus had the vital fluids sucked from His body by the intense rays of the sun. His condition was critical. While one can live for many days without food, one cannot survive nearly as long without water. Jesus was being deprived of crucial, life-sustaining water. His human body ached for what it needed to survive. His suffering was intense and excruciatingly painful.

III. Insistence on Obeying Scripture

"Later, knowing that all was now completed, and so that the Scripture would be fulfilled, Jesus said, 'I am thirsty'" (v. 28). Later . . . perhaps after John had taken Mary home and returned to the cross . . . and moreso, after the darkest hours of His suffering . . . when everything the Cross was intended to do was accomplished—only then did Jesus utter this word from the cross. Jesus had fulfilled every prophecy related to His role in God's redemptive process. In fact, the entire life of Christ was a fulfillment of Old Testament Scripture.

Matthew records 163 such fulfillments; Mark, 79; Luke, 150; and John, 49. Throughout Scripture the phrase *"that it might be fulfilled"* occurs with great frequency. Jesus did nothing that conflicted with God's prophetic Word—not even in His agonizing death.

IV. Identity with Us

It is of insurmountable comfort to realize that because of Christ's enduring everything that He did, He is supremely able to identify with us and to understand all our hurts and needs.

- Have you experienced suffering and adversity? So did Jesus.

- Have you experienced being separated from loved ones? So did Jesus.

- Have you experienced a broken heart? So did Jesus.

- Have you experienced being left out, overlooked, or forsaken? So did Jesus.

- Have you experienced physical pain? So did Jesus.

- Have you struggled with strong temptations? So did Jesus.

- Have you walked life's most difficult paths? So did Jesus.

Jesus went beyond what we experience in this life. He chose to experience the total wrath of God's judgment that we, as believers, will never know after death. When Jesus said, "I am thirsty," it was indicative of His passing through the fires of hell, paying the sin debt of mankind. The judgment He bore for those whom He saved through Calvary is beyond our capacity to imagine.

A small point of reference might be the suffering of the "rich man" in hell, from the story, told by Jesus, of this man and

Lazarus (Luke 16:19–31). In agony, the rich man cried out, "Father Abraham, have pity on me and send Lazarus to dip the tip of his finger in water and cool my tongue, because I am in agony in this fire" (v. 24). Apparently, he knew some of the thirst Jesus experienced as He descended into hell.

V. Indication of Universal Need

It is easy to see the universality of man's thirst for power, position, pleasure, and the pursuit of knowledge. Man's thirst never seems quenched. "More and then more" is the consuming desire that nothing seems to satisfy.

An article about entrepreneur Donald Trump appeared in the newspaper some years ago. It was the account that was published about the time of his divorce from Ivana, to whom he had been married for about thirteen years. In the article, Trump cited the deaths of three of his executives in a helicopter crash as one of the factors in his decision to end his marriage. The crash showed him "how short and how fragile life is." He told the interviewer, "I'm not the world's happiest person."

Trump's thirst for and achievement of power, position, and success are legendary. But according to this article, he had not found complete fulfillment and happiness in his accomplishments. He desired more from life. His story—albeit on quite a grandiose, storybook scale—is universal. Humankind always thirsts for more.

We thirst, but too often we look in the wrong places to be satisfied. The thirst comes from deep within our soul. If people are not regenerate—born again—they thirst to *be* God, at least

God of their life. This is universal. That thirst, however, will never be satisfied. If, on the other hand, a person is a born-again child of God, taste buds change and begin to thirst for something much more satisfying—the living water of Jesus Christ.

Jesus addressed this thirst when He spoke with the Samaritan woman at the well. Knowing she and her people needed to look beyond themselves and their world for fulfillment, He informed her: "Everyone who drinks this water will be thirsty again, but whoever drinks the water I give him will never thirst. Indeed, the water I give him will become in him a spring of water welling up to eternal life" (John 4:13–14).

For those who believe in Him as Lord and Savior, satisfaction of all thirsts will be theirs in heaven. "Never again will they hunger; never again will they thirst" (Rev. 7:16). Jesus is the Living Water.

Conclusion

Jesus said, "Blessed are those who hunger and thirst for righteousness, for they will be filled" (Matt. 5:6). We as believers participate in the Lord's Supper as an act of righteous obedience to our Master who commanded our devoted presence at His meal. As we partake of this sacred feast, let our hunger and thirst be for righteousness—right living with God and with our fellow man. As we hold the cup, let our thirst be for Him and His sovereign control of our lives. As we come to His Table, let us give thanks for the Living Water that graciously satisfies all our needs.

Contributed by Jim Henry
First Baptist Church, Orlando, Florida

Sermon 5:
General

TITLE: "Abusing and Misusing the Lord's Supper" [see chap. 8, Service 9]

SCRIPTURE: 1 Corinthians 11:17–34

- Christ instituted two ordinances: baptism and the Lord's Supper.

- Christ initiated Communion during the Passover meal.

- Paul established these ordinances at Corinth.

- The early church was distinguished by four marks: (1) Apostolic teaching, (2) prayer, (3) fellowship, and (4) breaking of bread (Acts 2:42).

I. Rebuke (vv. 17–22)

It is evident that this is very important to the Lord, as He gave considerable discussion to it. In Corinth, the Lord's Supper had degenerated. Why?

A. Division (vv. 18–19)
1. *Factious members were causing division* (v. 18).
   (a) "'I follow Paul'; another, 'I follow Apollos'; another 'I follow Cephas'; still another, 'I follow Christ,'" (1 Cor. 1:12).

(b) Differences: not doctrinal, but heretical

2. *Faithful members were having God's approval* (v. 19).

B. Confusion (vv. 20–22)
1. *Celebration practice was "not the Lord's Supper"* (v. 20).

2. *Celebration promoted disunity, rather than unity.*

II. Revelation (vv. 23–26)

Paul issues the corrective.

A. Obligation (vv. 23–24)
1. *"Received from the Lord"* (v. 23). Paul received a direct revelation from heaven that gave significant instructions on the correct observance of the Lord's Supper.

2. *"Do this . . . "* (v. 24). Paul related a divine command from the lips of the Lord Himself. Sharing in the Lord's Supper is not an option. Not to partake of holy communion is disobedience and sin.

B. Contemplation (vv. 24–25)
1. *"In remembrance . . . " To contemplate* means to "consciously call to mind."

2. *"For you."* These are two of the most beautiful words in the Bible! Substitutionary atonement *for you,* achieved in the death of the spotless Lamb of God, is the recollection to be celebrated in the Lord's Supper.

C. Proclamation (v. 26)

To proclaim means to preach. Every time we observe the Lord's Supper, we are preaching a sermon. Our obedience in partaking of Communion communicates more effectively than the persuasive words of any preacher of our relationship with the Lord.

D. Expectation (v. 26)

We celebrate the Lord's Supper expectantly *until He comes.* While it looks backward to His cross, it likewise looks forward to His crown. This observance is not only retrospective in its essence, but also prospective.

III. Reminder (vv. 27–34)

Paul gives instructions on how to approach the Lord's Table. There is much misunderstanding about the phrase, "in an unworthy manner" (v. 27). Many are apprehensive about their worthiness to receive Communion. We must remember our approach to the Lord's Table is not by our worthiness, but rather through the meritorious access of Jesus Christ.

A. Personal Inventory (vv. 28–32)

1. *"Examine himself"* (vv. 28, 31–32). We are called to examine ourselves before we come to His meal. If we judge our unworthiness, confess our sin, and examine our relationship with God and others, we are much better prepared to eat of the sacred feast.

2. *"Judgment on himself"* (vv. 29–30). This refers to chastening.

   a. "Weak." This is the condition in which one is left after a long exhausting illness.

   b. "Sick." This is the condition in which one is without health, and also one is unable to move speedily.

   c. "Fallen asleep." The term *asleep* refers to the death of a believer. In this passage, it refers to a believer's premature death.

B. Proper Consideration (vv. 33–34)

Our meeting together in worship and properly observing the Lord's Supper are important considerations for us who seek unity in the body of Christ. We are called to selfless obedience in how we carry out the Lord's commands.

Conclusion

- The Lord's Supper is a look back (vv. 23–26a).

- It is a look ahead (v. 26b).

- It is a look within (vv. 27–28, 31–32).

- It is a look around (vv. 33–34).[5]

Contributed by Jim Henry
First Baptist Church, Orlando, Florida

Sermon 6:
General

TITLE: "The Most Meaningful Memorial in the World" [see chap. 8, Service 10]

SCRIPTURE: 1 Corinthians 11:17–30

Memorials are an important part of our culture.

- *Historical reminders:* Washington Monument, Lincoln Memorial, Vietnam Memorial.

- *Visual reminders:* corporate logos, (e.g., the golden arches of McDonald's, the interlocking rings of the Olympics, the bold check of Nike).

- *Most recognizable symbols over the past fifty years:* Mickey Mouse ears, Coca-Cola logo, Swastika emblem.

- *Christians symbols:* ichthus, dove, cross.

- *God's Old Testament memorials:* rainbow, ark of the covenant, Jacob's well.

The Lord's Supper is a memorial instituted by God in honor of Jesus Christ, who gave His life for our sin.

- It is readily accessible to all believers.

- It is participatory for all who partake.

I. Look back and Remember
"Do this in remembrance of me" (v. 24)

A. Christ's body was broken for us.

1. No bone in His body was broken.

2. His body was pierced from head to toe.

B. Christ's blood was shed for us.

1. The sacrifices of the Old Testament were types of the atoning death of the Messiah.

2. Without the shedding of His blood, there would be no forgiveness of sin.

II. Look within and Repent
"A man ought to examine himself" (v. 28)

A. Communion is not a time to examine others.

B. Communion is a time for examining ourselves.

1. Self-examination reveals our sin.

2. Self-examination encourages repentance.

3. Self-examination underscores the need for God's grace.

III. Look ahead and Rejoice
"You proclaim the Lord's death until He comes" (v. 26).

A. The Lord's Supper is not just a memorial; it is a celebration.

　1. Jesus Christ did not remain in the grave; He is alive.

　2. Jesus Christ is not only alive; He's going to return some day.

B. Every time we participate in Communion, we proclaim our hope of His return to the world.

A family at the end of our street kept their Christmas lights burning beyond Christmas and into the months of January and February. We didn't understand why, until finally in February a sign was placed outside their home. It read, "Welcome Home, Jimmy!" We then understood. Their son was returning from the Vietnam War.

The family kept their Christmas lights burning in anticipation of their son's return home. They were excited about celebrating Christmas together as a reunited family, and they wanted everyone to know. Likewise, when believers, as the family of God, celebrate the Lord's Supper, they announce to the world that they believe Jesus is alive and anticipate His coming again.

Contributed by Bob Russell
Southeast Christian Church, Louisville, Kentucky

Sermon 7:
General

TITLE: *"This Do Ye"* [see chap. 8, Service 11]

SCRIPTURE: 1 Corinthians 11:23–28

The observance of the Lord's Supper is one of the most important services in the church.

- It is important because Jesus commanded it (1 Cor. 11:24–25).

- It is important because the early church practiced it (Acts 2:42).

- It is important because today's believers focus on the heart of the gospel, the Cross (1 Cor. 2:2; Heb. 9:22).

- It is important because it is designed as a teachable moment when our whole being—mind, soul and body—is involved (Luke 24:39).

I. The Supper Is a Time of Remembrance of the Past (v. 24)

A. The Lord's Supper replaced the Passover meal, which called to remembrance God's deliverance of His people from Egypt.

B. Every action and each element of food had a purpose.

1. The lamb was killed at the temple, where the blood was poured out as a sin offering.

2. Unleavened bread represented the haste in which the Israelites left Egypt.

3. The bowl of salt water represented the tears of slavery and also the Israelites' passing over the Red Sea.

4. Bitter herbs represented the bitter life of slavery.

5. A paste of mashed fruit and nuts reminded them of bricks of clay made without straw.

6. The singing of Psalms 113–118 and Psalm 139 reminded the people that it was God who saved and blessed them.

7. Four cups of wine were poured to remind the Israelites of the four promises of God as found in Exodus 6:6–7.

C. In this time of remembrance, we remember Jesus.

1. Remember Jesus' life.

   a. His miraculous birth.

   b. His sinless life.

   c. His authoritative teachings.

2. Remember Jesus in His death (v. 26).

   a. His betrayal (Luke 22:21).

   b. His night of agony at Gethsemane (Matt. 26:38; Luke 22:44).

   c. His night of desertion (Mark 14:50).

   d. His night of trial.

   e. His night of beatings, interrogation, mockery, scourging, and bearing the cross.

II. The Supper Is a Time of Unity and Fellowship of the Present (1 Cor. 11:24; Acts 2:42)

A. The Lord's Supper is a present spiritual fellowship of the church as the family of God.

B. The Lord's Supper is a present communion of believers (1 Cor. 10:16–17).
The word *communion* is derived from the Greek word for *fellowship.*

C. The Lord's Supper is a present display of oneness among all believers who eat and drink of the body of Christ, and who share the spirit of this Supper (Acts 20:7).

D. The Lord's Supper is a present time for personal examination (vv. 27–28).

III. The Lord's Supper Is a Time of Anticipation of the Future (v. 26)

A. The Lord's Supper reminds us of the past and calls us to commitment in the present, so we may more fully anticipate Jesus' future coming in glory (1 Cor. 11:26; Mark 14:24–25).

B. The Lord's Supper anticipates our future presence at the wedding feast of the Lamb, when Jesus will be physically present with us (Rev. 19:7–9).

Conclusion

- The Supper is to help us remember the price paid for our salvation.

- The Supper is to remind us of the precious fellowship of the present.

- The Supper is to remind us of the future heaven God has prepared for us.

- The Supper is a supper of invitation to repentance and salvation.

Contributed by Roy T. Edgemon
Director, Discipleship and Family Development Division, Baptist Sunday School Board, Nashville, Tennessee

Sermon 8:
General

TITLE: *"The Significance of the Supper"*

SCRIPTURE: 1 Corinthians 11:23–34

I. The Institution of the Lord's Supper (vv. 23–26)

A. The Practice of It (v. 23)
- Receive
- Deliver

B. The Parts of It (vv. 23–25)
- The Bread
- The Cup

C. The Point of It (vv. 24,26)
- *"In remembrance"*
- *In obedience*

D. The Perpetuation of It (v. 26)
- *"Until . . ."*

II. The Intention of the Lord's Supper (v. 27)

- *"Unworthy manner"*

A. Time of Reflection

B. Time of Repentance

C. Time of Restoration

III. The Inspection at the Lord's Supper (vv. 28–34)

A. Personal (v. 28)

B. Priority (vv. 29–30)

C. Promising (v. 31)

D. Parental (v. 32).
- God the Father loves and disciplines His children.

E. Preferential (vv. 33–34)

Contributed by Jerry Sutton
Two Rivers Baptist Church, Nashville, Tennessee

Sermon 9:
General

TITLE: *"This Do Remembering Him"* [see chap. 8, Service 12]

SCRIPTURE: 1 Corinthians 11:23–32

Focus on three important truths related to the Lord's Supper in this text:

1. The *source* of the Supper is not a tradition or apostolic opinion, but rather the revelation given Paul directly from the Lord.

2. The *setting* of the Supper is the night of betrayal. Our Father set this beautiful Supper against the backdrop of supreme ugliness—the betrayal of His Son. This setting heightens the contrast between His gracious provision and man's bondage to sin.

3. Most importantly, the *Son* of the Supper, who gave Himself as the perfect sacrifice.

I. The Purpose of the Supper (v. 28)

A. Personal Examination
1. Disciples at the Last Supper were concerned about their personal commitment (Matt. 26:22).

2. Believers today are called to a time of personal examination (2 Cor. 13:5; Gal. 6:4).

B. Personal Consecration

Our personal examination should lead us to *personal consecration* (Ps. 139:23–24).

II. The Preparation for the Supper (vv. 27–32)

A. Conviction of Unworthy Communion

1. *Analyzed* (v. 27a). How is the Lord's Supper taken in an *unworthy manner*?

a. By ignoring it or saying it's unimportant.

b. By failing to observe it meaningfully.

c. By assuming it in itself is sufficient to save an individual.

d. By refusing to confess and repent of sin.

e. By having a lack of respect and love for God or His children.

2. *Applied* (v. 27b). To dishonor our flag is to dishonor our country. To dishonor our Lord's body is to dishonor Christ Himself. The result is treating Jesus' unique life and death as something common and insignificant.

3. *Avoided* (v. 28). As believers, we should not avoid rigorous self-examination. We need to be certain we are not careless, flippant, indifferent, unrepentant, or irreverent when we partake of the Lord's Supper.

B. Consequences of Unworthy Communion (vv. 29–32)

1. *Reason for chastening* (vv. 29, 32). The word *judged* in verse 32 can be translated "chastised." God the Father

disciplines His children to correct their sinful behavior and to direct them in the paths of righteousness (Heb. 12:7)

   2. *Results of chastening* (vv. 30–31)
     a. Administered (v. 30)
     b. Avoided (v. 31)

C. Cost of Unworthy Communion (vv. 24–25)

   1. *Seen in the bread* (v. 24). The unleavened bread had long been a symbol of God's chosen people leaving Egypt and their past behind. Leaven symbolized influence. The unleavened bread was a way of saying, "We are starting anew. Our old life will not influence us." Unleavened bread symbolizes Christ's body as well as our old life left behind.

   2. *Seen in the blood* (v. 25). God required the shedding of blood when making a covenant with man (Heb. 9:28). Once a year, on the day of atonement, a perfect, spotless lamb's blood was shed to cover man's sin and man's breaking of God's covenant (Heb. 10:14). John the Baptist declared Jesus was "the Lamb of God, who takes away the sin of the world!" (John 1:29).

Conclusion

Our desire in observing the Lord's Supper is to *remember Him.*

    Contributed by Johnny M. Hunt
    First Baptist Church, Woodstock, Georgia

Sermon 10:
General/Lenten

TITLE: *"The Cross: It Took Just One—Once"* [see chap. 8, Service 8]

SCRIPTURE: Hebrews 9:26

What Christ meant to do on the cross, He accomplished.

- He did not die in vain; He died with no part of His work left undone.

- He did not die to make us savable; He died to save us.

- He did not die that sin might be vanquished by some effort of our own; He died to vanquish sin Himself—once and forever.

One death.
    One sacrifice.
        One atonement.
            One cross.
The whole gospel was hung on the cross.

One price and purchase.
    One cross and crown.
        One death and deliverance.
            One, and only once.
The Savior said victoriously, "It is finished!"

I. One Person—"He"

Who was He?

- He was very God of very God.

- He was commissioned by the Father to vanquish sin (John 6:44).

- He was the Messiah, pledged by God's covenant to deliver His people (John 1:41).

- He was chosen (1 Pet. 1:20).

God didn't send a mighty angel.
　　He didn't send a mighty army.
　　　　He didn't send a mighty man.
　　　　　　He sent *His Son*—Himself.

II. One Period—"Appeared Once"

He appeared as a babe in Bethlehem;
　　The infinite linked with the Infant.
He who laid out the heavens,
　　Now lays upon a woman's breast.[6]

He invaded time and history.
He came as the God-Man.
He was unique.

　　No one was like Him in the past.
　　　　No one was like Him in the present.
　　　　　　No one would be like Him in the future.
He appeared once.

He is "Wonderful Counselor,
    Mighty God,
  Everlasting Father,
    Prince of Peace" (Isa. 9:6).
He is King of kings.
He chose not stay on His throne.
He came to earth for one brief period in time.

III. One Purpose—"To Do Away with Sin"

A. Sin and Its Presence
Sin is a reality for fallen man (Rom. 3:23).

B. Sin and Its Price
Sin cannot be tolerated by a just and holy God, as sin is contrary to His perfect nature.

1. *Separation and reconciliation.* Sin, producing enmity between God and man, requires atonement for the restoration of man's relationship with God (Rom. 5:10).

2. *Condemnation and satisfaction* (Rom. 5:18; 6:23; 8:1). Sin's satisfaction is what we celebrate as we gather at His Table. As we partake of the elements, representing His body and blood given in atonement for our sin, let us receive with assurance the benefits of His grace. As believers we have been redeemed and restored in our never-ending relationship with the Prince of Peace.

IV. One Payment—"Once for All . . . the Sacrifice"

In the Old Testament, the sacrifice was a personal, spiritual encounter with God. Sacrifices were offered to satisfy God, who was present in judgment and mercy. A blood sacrifice was demanded. This had to be repeated time and again.

Jesus' perfect sacrifice accomplished *"once for all"* all God demanded as the payment for our sin. No longer would other sacrifices be required. In holy Communion, we remember all Christ has accomplished for us in His sacrificial death.

Contributed by Jim Henry
First Baptist Church, Orlando, Florida

Sermon 11:
General

TITLE: *"The Precious Blood of Christ"* [see chap. 8, Service 13]

SCRIPTURE: 1 Peter 1:17–20

I. Predestined Blood (v. 20)

Before God created the universe—before the cosmos or the chaos came into being—God planned for the Cross. Jesus' death upon the cross was a divine appointment, not a devastating accident! God predestined or chose our redemption before the foundation of the world (Rev. 13:8; Acts 2:23).

The lamb is a central theme throughout God's Word and in God's redemption plan:

A. The Necessity
  - In Genesis 4: Abel and his lamb.

B. The Provision
  - In Genesis 22: Abraham and his lamb (Isaac's substitute).

C. The Slaying
  - In Exodus 12: Passover lamb.

D. The Character
  - In Leviticus: Sin-offering lamb (sacrificed on the altar outside the tabernacle).

E. The Person
- In Isaiah 53: Suffering lamb (prophesied).

F. That Person
- In John 1:29–36: The Lamb of God (announced by John the Baptist).

G. That Promised Christ
- In Acts 8: The slaughtered Lamb (as proclaimed in God's Word, which led to the Ethiopian eunuch's conversion).

H. The Enthronement
- In Revelation 5: The enthroned Lamb.

I. The Kingship
- In Revelation 21–22: The reigning Lamb.

II. Precious Blood (v. 19)

One would not expect such a rugged fisherman as Simon Peter to use the descriptive term *precious*. Yet his use of *precious* is recorded four times in 1 Peter and twice in 2 Peter. What is it that Peter calls "precious"? It is the "precious blood of the Lamb." Christ's blood was never called "precious" until after Calvary. *Precious* has a twofold meaning:

A. Precious in Value (Acts 20:28).

Robert Lowry, in 1876, wrote the hymn text:

Oh! Precious is the flow,
That makes me white as snow.
No other fount I know;
Nothing but the blood of Jesus.

Frances Havergal saw a picture of the crucified Christ with the caption, "I did this for thee. What hast thou done for me?" She wrote a poem based on the caption. Dissatisfied with the way it turned out, she tossed the poem into the fireplace. Amazingly it came out of the fireplace—unburned! Her father suggested that she have this poem published:

> I gave my life for thee,
> My precious blood I shed,
> That thou might ransomed be,
> And quickened from the dead.
> I gave, I gave, my life for thee,
> What hast thou given for me?

This *precious blood of the Lamb* is of infinite value. Its price was greater than any price previously paid. It cost the very Son of God His own blood in perfect sacrifice.

B. Precious in Rarity

Years ago, the Rockefeller Report gave an account of a West African named Acebe, who supplied from his veins the very first blood from which the vaccine for yellow fever was derived. Acebe contracted yellow fever but miraculously recovered. This made the antibodies in his blood precious to those who were seeking a cure for this deadly disease. Acebe allowed his blood to be taken for this life-giving purpose.

In 1937, the yellow fever vaccine was first manufactured from that one man's blood. The original strain of the virus obtained from that humble man has gone throughout the earth—from laboratory to laboratory, from hospital to hospital—providing immunity for millions. The Rockefeller

Foundation stated that through science, the blood of one man in West Africa had been made to serve the whole human race.

The untainted blood of only one man could provide the cure for an epidemic known as sin that had been attacking the human race since the time of Adam. Only one man, the *precious Lamb of God,* could yield the cure—not by donating *some* blood, but by shedding it all in His sacrificial death on the cross.

III. Pure Blood (v. 19)

A. The Lamb was Chosen for Its Perfection (Deut. 15:21).

In choosing the Passover lamb, Jews selected "a lamb without blemish or defect." The healthiest, finest-looking yearling was singled out from the rest of the flock. This lamb was at the prime of its life—still frisky and adorable. It then was carefully observed for four days before the Passover to make sure it was healthy and perfect in every way. By the end of the fourth day, the lamb usually had won the affection of the entire household—especially that of the children. This made it particularly difficult as the time came for the head of the household to slay the lamb they had grown to love.

Likewise, the Lamb of God was *without blemish or defect.* When Christ was accused and on trial before Pontius Pilate, no fault was found in Him.

B. The Lamb Was Chosen for Death (Isa. 53:7–9)

The perfect Lamb was marked for death to cover the sins of the people (Isa. 53:9).

C. The Lamb Was Chosen to Have No Bone Broken in It

As the Passover lamb had no bone broken in it, the Lamb of God had no bone broken by the Roman soldiers who customarily broke the legs of those crucified.

D. The Lamb Was Chosen for Preparation with Fire

The Passover lamb was prepared by being roasted with fire. The Lamb of God prepared to take away the sins of the world by facing God's judgment in the fires of hell (2 Cor. 5:21). In response to this judgment, Jesus cried, "My God, my God, why have you forsaken me?" (Matt. 27:46).

IV. Powerful Blood (vv. 18–19)

The powerful blood of Christ is redeeming for those who are covered by it. Like the blood of the Passover lamb, the blood of the Lamb of God has four powerful characteristics:

A. Saving

It was the *blood* of the lamb that saved the Hebrews in the Passover (Exod. 12:23): "Take a bunch of hyssop, dip it into the blood in the basin and put some of the blood on the top and on both sides of the doorframe. Not one of you shall go out the door of his house until morning" (Exod. 12:22). The basin to which the verse refers is not a container but a ditch dug in front of the doorways to avoid the flooding of homes. The Israelites killed their Passover lambs right by the doors, letting the blood from the slaughter run into the depression. Using a brush made of hyssop, they painted the blood on the doorway.

They first touched the lintel, the top horizontal part of the doorframe, and then they painted each doorpost. In doing so, they went through the motions of making the sign of a bloody cross. The door was sealed on all four sides by the blood of the lamb. The blood above the door foreshadowed the thorns that crushed Christ's brow. The blood on either side foreshadowed His nail-pierced hands. The blood below foreshadowed His nail-pierced feet.

The King James translation of John 10:9 reads, "I am the door: by me if any man enter in, he shall be saved, and shall go in and out, and find pasture." The Israelites entered the blood-stained door and were saved. The next morning, they departed for good pastures, the Promised Land.

What if some Hebrew had tried to save himself by adorning his door with gold or silver or jewels instead of blood? He would have been foolish. Likewise, if we try to save ourselves through good works, baptism, the Lord's Supper—anything other than simple faith in the atoning blood of Jesus Christ—we, too, are foolish (1 Pet. 1:19).

B. Secure (Exod. 12:3–7,12–13)

The Hebrew verb meaning "to pass over" means more than stepping or leaping over something in order to avoid contact with it. The phrase has no connection with any other Hebrew word, but it does bear resemblance to an Egyptian word, *pesh.* This word means "to spread wings over" (in order to protect).

In the Passover, the Lord was not merely passing by the houses of the Israelites. Rather, He was standing guard—protecting each home covered by the blood of the lamb from the wrath of the destroying angel. All those in the Hebrew households were safe from death's path.

A Christian martyr was summoned before the authorities: "You are a heretic! You will be damned!" The martyr boldly expressed his faith in Christ: "No. Therefore, there is now no condemnation to them that believe in Christ Jesus!" This martyr knew, as the hymn writer did, that, he was "safe in the arms of Jesus."

C. Sufficient

As the blood of the Passover lamb was sufficient to cover the sins of the Israelite household, so, too, the blood of Christ is sufficient to cover all our sins (1 John 1:9).

D. Sanctifying

1. *Cleanses.* There is a simple experiment you can perform to grasp the function of the blood as a cleansing agent. Find a blood pressure test kit and wrap the cuff around your upper arm. When it is in position, have someone pump it up to about 200 mm of mercury. Initially your arm will feel an uncomfortable tightness beneath sufficient pressure to stop the flow of blood in your arm. Now comes the revealing part of the experiment: perform any easy task with your cuffed arm. Merely flex your fingers and make a fist about ten times in succession or cut paper with scissors or drive a nail into wood with a hammer.

The first few moments will seem quite normal as the muscles obediently contract and relax. Then you will feel a slight weakness. Almost without warning, a hot flash of pain will strike after about ten movements. Your muscles will cramp. If you force yourself to continue the simple task, you will likely cry out in agony. Finally, you cannot will yourself to continue. The pain overwhelms you.

When you release the tourniquet and air escapes the cuff, blood will rush into your aching arm, and a wonderful sense of relief will soothe your muscles. The pain is worth enduring just to experience the acute relief. Your muscles move freely, the pain vanishes, and all feels good again. Physiologically, you have just experienced the cleansing power of blood.

While the blood supply to your arm was shut off, you forced your muscles to keep working. As they converted oxygen to energy, they produced certain waste products (metabolites) that are normally flushed away instantly in the bloodstream. Due to the constricted blood flow, however, these metabolites accumulated in your cells. They were not "cleansed" by the swirling stream of blood, and therefore, in a few minutes you felt the agony of retained toxins.

Blood sustains life by carrying away the chemical by-products that would interfere with the body's healthy processes. Forgiveness through Jesus Christ's shed blood cleanses life's waste products—sin that impedes true health—just as blood cleanses harmful metabolites (1 John 1:7).[7]

2. *Replaces.* In addition to removing sin, Christ's blood replaces it with his righteousness(2 Cor. 5:21).[8]

Near the end of his life, François Mauriac, the French Catholic novelist who received the Nobel Prize for literature, reflected on his own love-hate history with the church. He detailed the ways in which the church had not kept its promise: the petty rifts and compromises that have characterized it throughout history. The church, he said, had strayed far from the precepts and example of its founder. And yet, added Mauriac, despite all its failings, the church had at least remembered two words of Christ: "Your sins are forgiven you" and "This is my body broken for you."[9]

The Lord's Supper brings together those two "words" of Christ in a meaningful ceremony of remembering the sufficiency and sacrifice of His shed blood and receiving the cleansing benefits of His grace.

Contributed by Jim Henry
First Baptist Church, Orlando, Florida

Sermon 12:
Lenten/Maundy Thursday/General

TITLE: *"The Upper Room: A Time to Remember"* [see chap. 8, Service 15]

SCRIPTURE: Luke 22:8

The arrangements had been made. The room in which to eat the meal had been secured. The food for the feast had arrived. The group, consisting of a leader and twelve of His close followers, was present to celebrate an event that had happened about twelve hundred years prior.

The main purpose of the gathering was to remember. The people felt that God had broken through time and history in a dramatic way to help His people gain their freedom from the oppressive bonds of servitude to the Egyptians. In gratitude, God's people should never forget God's deliverance. A special time, therefore, was set aside yearly to remember.

Remembering was—and still is—a dominant characteristic of Jewish religious observances. One of the interesting aspects of this time of remembrance was the personalizing of God's redemption. The individual Jew felt it was not just some ancient ancestor who participated in the Exodus, the Red Sea crossing, the desert wandering, or the entrance into the Promised Land. Rather, the individual felt it had likewise happened to him. With such a mind-set, Jews were personally engaged in remembering God's love, mercy, and guidance. Through observance of the Sabbath and religious festivals, successive generations of Jews became aware of their heritage and—above all else—the God who had brought them out of bondage into the Promised Land.

Even today among Israelites, remembering is highly prioritized. Every army officer takes an oath of allegiance on Masada, the Dead Sea fortress where 960 Jewish zealots committed suicide rather than being taken captive by the Romans. And the message is: *Remember Jewish patriotism! Remember heroic service! Remember it is better to die than to be taken captive!* Likewise, the museum of the Holocaust has a similar message: *Remember the six million Jews who lost their lives under Hitler's regime! Remember, and be certain it never happens again!*

I. A Time to Remember Christ, the Covenant-Giver

Jesus gave His followers—then and now—a new reason to remember. Through Jesus Christ, God established a new covenant with His people—Jewish and Gentile believers—that provided a means of forgiveness that went far beyond the old sacrificial system of the Jews. In this new covenant, people would know the depth of God's love and the length to which He would go to assure people of His desire to have a personal relationship with them. The cross was squarely in the middle of the upper room. In a few hours, it would facilitate Jesus' body being broken and His blood being shed.

II. A Time to Remember Christ, the Servant

After walking the dusty roads of Palestine, a guest had his feet washed upon entering a home. This considerate gesture was usually performed by a household servant. This was the role assumed by Jesus as He tied a towel around His waist and washed the feet of His disciples. It has been suggested that if a Christian was issued a uniform of the faith, it would include a towel to go about the waist. This towel would serve as a reminder of Jesus' humbling Himself as a servant, and of the Christian's need to do likewise. Let us remember: no task is too menial or too lowly for one enlisted to serve under Christ's command.

III. A Time to Remember Christ, the Betrayed

The events of the upper room should also cause us to remember a third thing about Christ: His announcement to His disciples that one of them would betray Him. Jesus' declaration met with the immediate question, "Lord, is it I?" by disciple after disciple.

When it comes to the realization that by word, attitude, or deed we, too, are capable of betraying Christ, we need to search our souls prayerfully. Is it I who has been unappreciative of what Christ has done for me? Is it I who has failed to accept Christ's offer of forgiveness, help, and empowerment? Is it I who—by my not being faithful to my vow to surrender to His Lordship—have betrayed Christ?

Conclusion

The Lord's Table is most certainly a time to remember:
- to remember Jesus established the basis of my restored relationship with God;

- to remember Jesus calls me to follow His example of being a servant to others;

- to remember I need to search my soul lest denial—or even betrayal—be found there;

- to remember that, through faith, I can know the certainty of fellowship and eternal life with Jesus Christ.

Contributed by Charles A. Graves
United Methodist minister, Spartanburg, South Carolina

Sermon 13:
Labor Day/General

TITLE: *"The Power of Spiritual Memory"* [see chap. 8, Service 16]

SCRIPTURE: Deuteronomy 8:6–18; 1 Corinthians 11:23–31; 2 Corinthians 1:20–22

NOTE: *Begin this meditation by placing an open laptop computer in front of the speaker in view of the congregation.*

The computer has become an essential part of modern life. Wherever one goes, one may stay in touch with work, whims, and the World Wide Web. For many, the laptop is as necessary for survival in today's world as the telephone or television. In a very real sense, the computer has become the core of the information age. For many, it is the symbol of their labor.

Labor used to be symbolized by a hard hat, the utility belt, a tool, or some sort of machinery related to the factory experience. In fact, Labor Day has its roots in the Industrial Age of America. In that era, a tremendous amount of strain and toil went into the hot and long workdays of summer. Because of this, a day was designated to honor laborers in the first month of autumn. Labor Day gave these workers a break from the heat and the strain and an opportunity to be reinvigorated to reach maximum productivity in the fall months.

Today we continue to celebrate Labor Day. Although we have lessened the physical strain on the average worker, we have increased the mental stress in this fast-paced information age. While the critical issue in the Industrial Age was machinery, the crucial requirement of the Information Age is memory.

How much memory is available? The amount of memory available in a computer has much to do with the speed, intensity, and opportunity one has to access the information needed to accomplish tasks. The greater the memory, the greater the speed, efficiency, and productivity in one's labor. This attentiveness to memory—which has become the hallmark of the information age—is nothing new. In Deuteronomy, God addresses this subject of memory and its importance.

I. Measure Your Spiritual Memory (Deut. 8:6–18)

God told Israel of the importance of memory. He warned His people that when they possessed the abundant blessings of the Promised Land, they were not to forget what He had done for them and what He, as the only true and holy God, demanded of them. It is God who is the Giver of "the ability to produce wealth" (v. 18).

It is as true for us today as it was for those Israelites: that it is not simply by the sweat of our brow or by the skill of our hands by which we acquire wealth and possessions (v. 17). We should not take pride in ourselves (v. 14), but rather, we should remember what God has done for us and praise Him for His rich blessings (v. 10).

II. Expand Your Memory (1 Cor. 11:23–26)

The New Testament also addresses the subject of memory and remembrance. We find this in the 1 Corinthians passage. In a very real sense, the Lord's Supper was given to us to expand our memory. It was inaugurated in order to keep us at the edge of God's blessing, so that we might begin to process all the blessedness of a life lived in obedience to God's covenants and in a personal relationship with the covenant mediator, Jesus Christ. We are called to remember that Jesus alone is the One who has accomplished the fullness and the blessedness of this covenant for us.

In remembering Christ at His Table, we first need to reflect on who Christ is and what He has done. We also should remember the moment of our conversion. The meaning of the Supper increases in direct proportion to our ability to remember what it was like to step out of the kingdom of darkness into the kingdom of light and life. Likewise, we need to remember His commandments, God's standards of obedience. Before we participate in His meal, we are called to examine our faithfulness to living as He commanded.

III. Upgrade Your Software (2 Cor. 1:20–22)

In this passage, we begin to see the implications of this covenant. We also begin to understand why there is so much power in spiritual memory. The power of the memory of what Christ has done for us is that, in Christ, all the promises of God have become a part of the software package available in your life. It is not by our strength, abilities, or goodness that we handle life's challenges, but rather it is by Jesus Christ that we have ready access to whatever resources, power, or wisdom we need. Through the power of a good memory of who Christ is and what He has done, we tap into the promises of God.

IV. Check for a Virus (1 Cor. 11:27–31)

There is one thing, however, that can prevent the maximum utilization of the blessings and power of God in our lives. It is identified in the Bible as an evil virus called sin. When this virus is harbored in our lives, it will take away, deform, and devour the spiritual memory of what Christ has done. In addition, it will destroy the program of God's blessing in our lives.

We need regularly to do a virus check on sin in order to allow the Holy Spirit to counteract its effect. This is essential for us to live continually in the fullness of God's blessings. So, as we come to the Lord's Table, we are called to check for available memory and for viruses in order to run properly God's program of grace.

There is at least one more thing we must remember: His cleansing. God's Word says, "If we confess our sins, he is faithful and just and will forgive us our sins and purify us from all unrighteousness" (1 John 1:9). Not *some* unrighteousness, *all* unrighteousness. Not *some* sins, *all* sin. We cannot take away the implications of our sin; however, what *we* cannot do to remove the virus of sin, *Jesus* has already done through the shedding of His blood. Because of the power of His blood, the virus has been rendered inoperative in the lives of believers. As we approach the Lord's Table, we must remember all He has done for us. Jesus said, "Do this in remembrance of me" (1 Cor. 11:24).

Contributed by David H. McKinley
First Baptist Church, Merritt Island, Florida

Sermon 14:
Thanksgiving

TITLE: *"Come to the Table"* [see chap. 8, Service 18]

SCRIPTURE: 1 Corinthians 11:23–29

Nothing can compare to that moment on Thanksgiving Day when those words for which we've waited all year are finally uttered: "Come to the table!" The house is filled with the delicious smell of hot-baked turkey and all the "fixin's." Traditional dishes carrying family memories are added, making the occasion one of the brightest moments of family celebration. The call to come implies several things—things, when reflected upon, prepare our hearts for gathering at the Lord's Table.

I. It Is an Invitation to Come Personally

It is an invitation and a command given to you: come. With this appeal, there are some assumptions made: your hands are clean, you have a good appetite, and you are ready to enjoy the meal. In much the same way, we prepare for the Table of our Lord.

A. We need clean hands.

We should never presume upon our host, to approach His Table without having "clean hands"—that is, having confessed our sins before the Lord.

B. We need a good appetite.

Just as sin will defile our hands, sin will take away an appetite for the things of God. Jesus said, "Blessed are those who hunger and thirst for righteousness, for they will be filled" (Matt. 5:6).

C. We need to take time to enjoy the moment.

A meal can never be truly enjoyed in a rush. Time needs to be set aside to enjoy a special occasion. The supper of our Lord is such a time for us. We should not overlook the importance of taking time to calm our hearts and linger at the table with Him.

Paul, in giving instructions for our preparation for the Lord's Table, said, "A man ought to examine himself" (1 Cor. 11:28). We come to the Lord's Table by His invitation and provision. We come in response to His grace. His Table is not one of merit, but one of mercy. Thus, we should examine ourselves to see if we are coming in faith to the Table, if we are coming "cleaned up" and prepared to partake of the meal.

II. It Is an Invitation to Come Collectively

We gather together as members of a family with a common life, a common love, and a collective identity. The Lord's Supper is a family feast for the church. While all must prepare individually, we share the meal and the moment collectively. The church is the family of God, the body of Christ, the Father's household. In Scripture, there is an emphasis on this meal's being a *shared experience* among fellow believers, not an individual act or ordinance (Acts 2:42–47).

III. It Is an Invitation to Come Expectantly

There is much awaiting you at the Lord's Table. You are to approach the feast with great expectations. The Lord said, "Man does not live on bread alone, but on every word that comes from the mouth of God" (Matt. 4:4). Jesus is the bread, satisfying all the hunger of our hearts. When we gather at the Lord's Table, there should be an expectancy not only about the meaningful experience of sharing the meal, but also about the promise of the return of the host Himself (Matt. 26:29; 1 Cor. 11:26).

IV. It Is an Invitation to Come Gratefully

On the night of the inaugural Lord's Supper, our Savior gave thanks (1 Cor. 11:24) and then broke and distributed the bread. For us, this gathering is a time to be thankful and to reflect on the goodness of God in our lives. In a most unique sense, the Lord's Supper is a Thanksgiving feast of our Savior, the Cross, and our salvation. We must never lose sight of the joy of coming to the Table and of gratefully receiving the favor of being seated with Him. When considering what Christ has accomplished through His suffering for me, the text of the hymn "The Wondrous Cross" seem the most appropriate expression.

Contributed by David H. McKinley
First Baptist Church, Merritt Island, Florida

Sermon 15:
Advent/Christmas

TITLE: *"A Christmas Communion"* [see chap. 8, Service 19]

SCRIPTURE: Luke 22:14–20; Luke 2:11–12, 15

There are many ways to recall who Jesus was and is—and what He did for us as Savior and Lord. Concerning His last meal with the disciples, Jesus said, "Do this in remembrance of me" (Luke 22:19). Henceforth, this meal has been a significant memorial of Christ's life on earth. The Lord's Supper is also a sign for each of us to remember Christ's death "in the flesh" for our sin.

It is most appropriate, therefore, at Christmas to celebrate this sacred meal combined with *the sign of the baby* in the manger—"The Word became flesh and made his dwelling among us" (John 1:14a); and *the sign of the Savior*—who was born to "be crucified and on the third day be raised again" (Luke 24:7); and the *sign of the King*—the risen and triumphant "King of kings and Lord of lords" (Rev. 19:16). His body and blood were in the manger, as well as on the cross and risen from the tomb.

I. Remember the Sign of the Baby

God through Jesus is always "being born" as believers are reborn to new life. The *baby in the manger* is a sign to recall what He did for us as Messiah. His mercies "are new every morning" (Lam. 3:23). Indeed, they are new this Christmas! Go to the manger! "Do this is in remembrance of me." The sign of salvation has come in birth of Jesus Christ.

II. Remember the Sign of the Savior

The babe in the manger cries out for us to remember God who became like us—to save us (Heb. 4:15). The God of all creation humbled Himself. God Himself became a fragile baby to understand our weakness and to show us the way to overcome the world by the power of His Spirit, even unto death on the cross. Angels announced His being vulnerable for our sakes. The manger is a *sign of the Savior* and His amazing grace!

III. Remember the Sign of the King

The coming King "attacked" the world as a baby. He chose not armies—or a royal birth—to display His power. His strength, as ours, was made perfect in weakness; yet that "baby" won the victory at Calvary! Behold the manger. Remember the hymn writer's words: "This manger of Bethlehem cradles a King."

Conclusion

The celebration of Jesus' birth calls us to remember Him as the humble infant who was born on earth, so we might be reborn through His death and resurrection. The manger, like the Cross and the empty tomb, is a sign of His victory.

Contributed by William A. Pickett
Pine Castle United Methodist Church, Orlando, Florida

CHAPTER TEN

The Illustration

❖

A constant challenge to those who preach is applying God's Word in terms that are easily understood by those who are in the pews. Finding those "perfect" illustrations to engage the listeners is the quest of pastors week in and week out as sermons are prepared for delivery. I have kept a categorized filing system for illustrations over the years. In these files I place stories, anecdotes, and illustrations that I come across almost daily. In fact, others—knowing how much I enjoy telling a good story—have sent me clippings and articles for my files. The following illustrations are some of those that I have found effective in communicating the deep meaning of His Supper.

Christ and the Cross

Artist

An Italian artist named Francetti is said never to have completed a painting of Christ on the cross, because every time he tried to paint it he wept so hard he could not put his brush to the canvas.[10]

Crucial/Crux/Cross

That the Cross is of central importance to Christianity is clear even in the language we use. *Crucial* is derived from a Latin word meaning "pertaining to a cross." *Crux* is Latin for "cross." Whenever we say, "The crux of the matter is this," or "This is the crucial point," we are saying, "Just as the Cross is central to Christianity, so is the point central to my argument."[11]

New Ears

A pastor received a call from a new father. He wanted the pastor to be present when he told his wife she had given birth to a beautiful baby boy, healthy in every way, except the newborn had no ears.

The baby had auditory openings and all the inner ear parts necessary to receive sound, but no fleshly parts outside which we know as ears. The doctors assured the parents that the problem would be corrected when his growth was complete and a donor was found.

School was tough for the boy. Many times he came home crying, "I'm a freak!" He became aware of the stares, whispers, and taunts of the other kids. He grew up learning to live with this. He became an excellent student and entered college to study geology.

One day he received a call from his father saying, "Well, son, we've finally found a donor. The operation will be this summer."

Following the operation, he was so happy! His new ears were beautiful. He graduated with honors and moved to the

Midwest to work. One day he received a call from his dad saying, "Son, your mother has had a heart attack, please come home."

He soon arrived, only to learn that his mother had died. At the funeral home, his dad called him over to the casket, pushed back his dear mother's hair to show the son: his mother didn't have any ears!

This moving and true story brings to us an added dimension to the love of God. This mother gave a part of herself to her son who had a deep need. God gave not his ears, but His all, to us through His blessed Son.[12]

Pardoned through Love

During the life of Cromwell, a young soldier committed a grave offense and was condemned to die. The sentence was to be carried out on a certain day at the ringing of the curfew bell. It was the occasion of a double sorrow. The soldier was not only very young, he was also engaged to be married to a beautiful girl. This young woman, who loved him dearly, tried in various ways to save his life, but her efforts failed. She even tried to bribe the sexton not to ring the bell, but again she failed.

The hour for the soldier's death drew near. He was brought forth; everyone waited for the bell to ring; but to the astonishment of all, the bell did not ring. The girl, unseen, had climbed to the belfry and seized the tongue of the bell. The bell ringer threw his weight upon the rope, and the great bell reeled to and fro in the tower. The noble girl held on, swinging with the bell, bruised, battered, and bleeding in her highly perilous position.

But the curfew bell did not ring that night.

When Cromwell heard the story, he immediately pardoned the guilty man. Surely, nothing would be too good for that young fellow to give to the one who loved him so wondrously and who risked her own life to save him.[13]

Likewise, Christ's love, as demonstrated by His death on the cross, brings pardon for the guilty. "And he died for all, that those who live should no longer live for themselves but for him who died for them and was raised again" (2 Cor. 5:15).

Trees

God had His first fellowship with man under the boughs of green forests in a beautiful garden. Adam stumbled over a tree. Noah built an ark of gopher wood. From a desert tree Moses shaped a pole, placed upon it a bronze serpent, and directed to it the dying gaze of a poisoned people.

The wilderness tabernacle,
    its table of shewbread,
        its sacrificial altar,
            its mercy seat, and
                the ark of the covenant

were God's instruments through which He taught His chosen people. Solomon built a temple for God from the cedars of Lebanon.

Jesus loved trees.
    They gave Him a manger in which to be born,
        a boat for a pulpit and a bed,
            a high tower of prayer on the mountaintop.

Branches of the palms added the only dignity to His entry into Jerusalem. In Gethsemane those sleepless sentinels kept their silent watch while the disciples slumbered.

Trees took Jesus over the water to His preaching missions,
    cooled His weary body in their soft shade,
        gave their fruit to His famished lips when He grew faint.

Then fingers of hate tore thorn branches from a tree and twined them into a mocking crown for His brow. Hands of scorn laid sharp steel to the roots of a forest monarch and shaped it into a shameful cross.

And then His freedom proclamation, "It is finished," found utterance from a tree. Man, the rebel, must be saved by grace. But trees have earned the right to immortality. Christ did not forsake His constant in His eternal city.

John, on the Isle of Patmos, glimpsed a wondrous sight and wrote, "In the midst of the street of it, and on either side of the river, there was THE TREE OF LIFE."[14]

Wounded Soldier

On March 15, 1985, Wayne Alderson—a successful labor negotiator from Pittsburgh—appeared on the *Today* show. The significance of the date was that it was the fortieth anniversary of Alderson's being wounded. He was the first American soldier to cross the Siegfried line into Germany in World War II. He had a permanent crease in his head from the wound.

Asked for his most important memory of the occasion,

Alderson replied that it was a redheaded friend who saved his life that day. Alderson had come face-to-face with a German soldier. The German threw a grenade at Alderson's feet, and Alderson shot the German. The grenade exploded almost instantly, sending Alderson to the ground, facedown in the mud.

A nearby German pillbox opened fire in his direction, and he knew that if the grenade had not killed him, the machine-gun fire would. But Alderson's redheaded friend turned him over, so he could breathe, and threw himself across his body, shielding him from the deadly fire.

"I can never forget the person who sacrificed his life to save me," said Alderson, tears in his eyes. "I owe everything to him. I can never forget . . . I owe everything to him."

God has shown us His love by Christ's death on the cross. We can never forget what He has done. We owe everything to Him.[15]

Forgiveness

Forgiven and Forgotten

In Hebrews 10:17 God says, "Their sins and lawless acts I will remember no more." Someone told the story of a bishop who was a confessor for a nun. The nun told him that Christ had revealed Himself to her in person. The bishop, understandably doubtful about her vision, said, "I have some instructions for you. The next time that Christ appears to you, I want you to ask Him about the sins of the archbishop."

The nun said, "Of course."

So the next time, in a period of confession, the bishop said to the nun, "Well, did you ask Christ about the sins of the archbishop?"

"Yes, I did, Father."

"Well, what did He say?"

And the nun answered, "He said, 'I've forgotten.'"

The living sacrifice of Jesus Christ reminds you of forgiveness. God has forgiven your sin on the cross.[16]

Ministry of Reconciliation

Simon Wiesenthal has committed much of his life to tracking Nazis guilty of war crimes. Although Wiesenthal himself survived the German concentration camps, he lost eighty-nine family members to the Nazis. He is often asked about his obsession: "Why hunt down men in their seventies and eighties for crimes committed half a century ago? Is there no forgiveness? No reconciliation with such people?" Wiesenthal set down his personal answers to such questions in a powerful book called *The Sunflower*. It begins with a haunting story, a remembrance of a true event that occurred during his imprisonment.

By chance, Wiesenthal was yanked out of a work detail and taken up a back stairway to a darkened hospital room. A nurse led him into the room, then left him alone with a figure wrapped in white, lying on a bed. The figure was a German soldier, badly wounded, swathed in yellow-stained bandages. Gauze covered his entire face.

In a weakened, trembling voice, the German made a kind of sacramental confession to Wiesenthal. He recounted his boyhood and early days in the Hitler youth movement. He told of action along the Russian front and the increasingly harsh measures an SS unit had taken against the Jewish populace.

And then he told of a terrible atrocity, when all the Jews in one town were herded into a wooden frame building that was then set on fire. Burning bodies fell from the second floor, and the SS soldiers—he among them—shot them as they fell. He started to tell of one child in particular—a young boy with black hair and dark eyes—but his voice gave way.

Several times Wiesenthal tried to leave the room, but each time the ghostlike figure would reach out with a cold, bloodless hand and beg him to stay. Finally, after maybe two hours, the soldier explained why Wiesenthal had been summoned. He had asked a nurse if any Jews still existed; if so, he wanted one brought to his room for a last rite before death.

"I know that what I am asking is almost too much for you," he said to Wiesenthal. "But without your answer I cannot die in peace." And then he asked for forgiveness for all his crimes against the Jews—from a man who perhaps the next day might die at the hands of the soldier's SS comrades. Wiesenthal stood in silence for some time, staring at the man's bandaged face. At last he made up his mind and left the room, without saying a word. He left the soldier in torment, unforgiven.

An old-fashioned theological word keeps cropping up in Wiesenthal's book. The word is *reconciliation.*

A profound phrase from the book of 2 Corinthians convinces me that we do have the right to offer forgiveness on behalf of another. In that passage, Paul announces that we have been granted "the ministry of reconciliation." "We are therefore Christ's ambassadors," he continues, "as though God were making his appeal through us. We implore you on Christ's behalf: Be reconciled to God" (2 Cor. 5:20).

The ethicists in Wiesenthal's book correctly note that forgiveness, grace, and reconciliation defy human reason. What logical right have I to offer forgiveness and reconciliation on someone else's behalf? Paul answers that question with this concluding statement, "God made him who had no sin to be sin for us, so that in him we might become the righteousness of God" (2 Cor. 5:21). The righteousness of God is an undeserved, "unreasonable" gift as well, a gift made possible only through Christ's own "ministry of reconciliation."[17]

Pardoned
For the Simonian family, the morning began like thousands of other mornings—with the juggling of bathroom privileges, dressing for another day's work, breakfast on the run. And then the telephone rang. The call it brought threw the family's schedule into a frenzy. In a half hour, President Bill Clinton would be stopping by to tour their produce market! You can imagine the panic that followed.

For three generations, since 1901, the Simonian family had operated a farm and a roadside stand, which had developed into a produce market. They had welcomed visitors from around the world, but never one with the prestige and power of the president of the United States. The visitor was important enough to justify the family's taking their youngest daughter, Ashley, out of school. How often does one get to shake hands with the current president—and on home ground?

Mr. Clinton and his entourage arrived on schedule. They toured the display of antique farm equipment. Cameras flashed as the president taste-tested the fresh kiwi, peaches, and succulent raisins. Every bite was a photo opportunity.

Before he resumed his tour of the valley, the president took out a pen and signed Ashley's memory book. He was then informed that she had skipped school in order to see him. So right there in the middle of the family produce market, Mr. Clinton invoked his powers as president of the United States. He wrote an official excuse for the girl to take to her teacher—a presidential pardon!

Presidential pardons have been issued for murderers, thieves, embezzlers, and derelict soldiers. But I imagine Ashley's pardon was a first in American history: a presidential pardon for absence from school. Regardless of his or her politics, it would be a rare teacher who would refuse to accept an excuse from one of the most powerful authorities on earth.

I imagine the girl's parents photocopied the handwritten excuse and gave the photocopy to the teacher, keeping the original in the family archives. I certainly would have. In fact, I would have put the document in a safety deposit box. Its cash value would increase with time. What a collector's item! What a gift to treasure! In years to come, I would proudly show my children the official pardon I had received from the forty-second president of the United States.

Come to think of it, I do possess a pardon—one that I treasure more than one written by a mere president. Mine is a pardon for my transgressions. It's not an excuse, for there is no excuse for my sins. And my pardon is not from my country's president, but from the Ruler of the universe. Whenever I reread my pardon, I'm filled with gratitude and praise (1 John 1:9; John 3:16).[18]

Reconciliation

A married couple had a history of bitterness and differences. It reached a peak one night when he announced that divorce was the only way out. She angrily said, "OK! I wish you'd go ahead!"

Within a week, he served her with papers. Since Satan really had a hold on them now, she began opening dresser drawers and throwing things into a suitcase. She declared she had "had it" and didn't want to be in the same house with him any longer. He sat in gloomy silence, realizing how awful the situation had become.

Unexpectedly, the woman opened one particular dresser drawer, and then she sank to her knees, sobbing uncontrollably. He instinctively went to her and saw what had brought on the flood of tears. Folded in one corner of the drawer were a few of the clothes of their daughter who had died some years before. The sight of those physical reminders of that precious child brought tears to his eyes as well.

Sinking to his knees beside her, the man embraced his wife, confessed his foolishness and sin, and asked her for forgiveness. She too admitted her fault, and they took turns tearing up the divorce papers. Reminders of the death of their child revived a love that had once united them and which could do so again.

When Christians who differ with one another redirect their gaze away from their own hurt feelings, selfish interests, or preconceived notions and look to the Cross where Jesus died for our selfishness, healing can begin. Through His death, reconciliation is possible.[19]

Repentance

What we need is forgiveness. In the movie *The Mission,* an eighteenth-century slavetrader, who murdered his blood brother in a fit of jealous rage, became a Jesuit in South America. In penance, he dragged through the mountainous jungle, by a rope tied to his neck, the heavy armor of his former life. He arrived in a Christian Indian village where, in the past, he had taken children by force from their mothers and husbands from their wives. One of the Indians rushed toward him with a knife—and cut the rope from his neck. The armor clanged down the mountainside; the forgiven murderer sobbed with joyful repentance. This is the forgiveness we need. This is what Jesus prayed for on Good Friday.[20]

Salvation

Dead to Sin

Have you ever been so sick that you thought you'd have to get better to die? Bruce Cummins of Bullhead City, Arizona, had just the opposite problem: he had to die in order to get better.

When Bruce checked into the hospital complaining of a severe headache, doctors discovered a cherry-sized aneurysm bulging near the base of his brain. An aneurysm is a sort of bubble in an artery. Eventually, that bubble ruptures. In Bruce's case, because the circulatory timebomb was so large and so close to the thinktank, its grenade-like effect would have meant instant death.

After consultation, the doctors opted for a radical procedure: they killed the patient—temporarily, of course. They chilled his body temperature from its normal 98.6 degrees to about 62, stopping heart and brain activity. For ten minutes or so, Bruce Cummins lay legally dead on an operating table. The aneurysm was snipped off, doctors jump-started his heart, and Cummins was brought back to life—and health.

I think this provides a vivid picture of what Paul is talking about in Romans 6. You and I have a sin problem of which the evident headaches are only symptoms. The aspirin of religion provides little relief and no cure. We have only one live option—to cease our struggles, lie beside Jesus in the tomb, and be declared dead. Only when we lie passive does the blood of Christ become active and raise us to eternal life. The symptoms of sin may linger for a while, but the source has been removed, "For he who has died is freed from sin."[21]

Doubly Indebted

A wealthy English family once invited friends to spend some time at their beautiful estate. The happy gathering was almost plunged into a terrible tragedy on the first day. When the children went swimming, one of them got into deep water and was drowning. Fortunately, the gardener heard them screaming and plunged into the pool to rescue the child. That youngster was Winston Churchill. His parents, deeply grateful to the gardener, asked what they could do to reward him. He hesitated, then said, "I wish my son could go to college someday and become a doctor." "We'll pay his way," replied Churchill's parents.

Years later when Sir Winston was prime minister of England, he was stricken with pneumonia. Greatly concerned, the king summoned the best physician who could be found to the bedside of the ailing leader. That doctor was Sir Alexander Fleming, the developer of penicillin. He was also the son of that gardener who had saved Winston from drowning as a boy! After his recovery, Churchill said, "Rarely has one man owed his life twice to the same person."

What was rare in the case of that great English statesman is in a much deeper sense a wonderful reality for every believer in Christ. The heavenly Father has given us the gift of physical life, and then through His Son, the Great Physician, He has imparted to us eternal life. We are doubly indebted to God as our Creator and Redeemer.[22]

Greatest Treasure

King Tut was fifteen or sixteen years old when he died, one of the richest kings the world had ever known. He wanted to hide his tomb because it contained wealth untold. There were four mummy cases of pure gold. All these cases had designs and figures on them. There were literally truckloads of precious stones, gold beads, bracelets, and trinkets placed in his tomb about four hundred miles south of Cairo, Egypt. At one time seven nations, including France, England, America, and Switzerland, were spending hundreds of thousands of dollars and many months looking for the tomb of King Tut.

On March 4, 1922, the crew of Howard Carter, an English-man, were digging in what is called the Valley of the Kings in Egypt, looking for that rich tomb. As they dug, they came across a smooth piece of cut stone. They called for Carter, say-ing, "Come here. We have found a smooth-cut stone buried deep back in the hill."

Howard Carter commanded that they continue the digging. They uncovered sixteen steps that led down to a masonry wall that had been there thousands of years, many years before Jesus walked on the earth. They took a large hammer and knocked out some of the masonry wall, revealing an opening. They knew then that they had discovered a tomb!

Howard Carter took a lighted candle and ran his arm through the opening, holding the light in the room. He saw the large tomb with inscriptions and writings all over the wall. After they knocked out more of the wall, Howard Carter ran his head through the hole and, without saying a word, took out the candle and pushed his head through the opening, turned and walked away a few feet.

His companion said to him, "Howard, what did you find?"

"The richest treasure in the world," he replied.

His companion said, "But you don't seem elated. Why aren't you more excited? This is what we came for. This is what we have been looking for!"

Howard Carter hung his head and said, "Twenty long, dirty, dusty, expensive years ago I dug within 72 inches of where we found the tomb today, yet I missed. That is why I am not happy."

My friends, there are people in our churches who are within one hundred feet of the most precious treasure to be found—the Cross of Calvary and God's plan of salvation that will lead them out of darkness into light. They need only to persevere in their search.[23]

Hidden Symptoms

In a European town, a man was not feeling good, so he went to the doctor for a checkup. After a thorough examination, the doctor could find nothing wrong. The man kept insisting there was something wrong, so he went to a second doctor and got a second checkup. This doctor also could find nothing wrong. Finally, the man went to a third doctor, insisting there was something wrong with him. After a complete physical, the doctor told the man there was nothing wrong with him physically.

But then the doctor said, "There is one thing wrong, however, but the prescription I will give you is rather unusual. All you need is just a good laugh. Although there is nothing wrong with you physically, you are so depressed, you seem to be carrying the weight of the world on your shoulders, and you have a frown on your face. All you need is just a good laugh. That would be the best thing that could happen to you. Here's what I want you to do. There is a circus in town with a clown named Cervantes. He has the reputation of being the 'world's funniest clown.' If you would go see him, I can promise you he will make you laugh."

At this, the patient began to walk out the door, worse off than he was when he came in. The doctor asked him, "What's the matter?" The man turned and looked at him and said, "That is impossible."

The doctor said, "Why is it impossible? The circus is just down the street. I took my whole family last night and we have never laughed so hard. Cervantes is the world's funniest clown. Why is it impossible?"

The man replied, "Doctor, the reason it is impossible is because I am Cervantes the clown."

Many people thought Cervantes was the happiest and funniest man in the world, yet something was wrong deep down inside. There are many people today who give the impression to others that everything is great. They act like they have it all together. They are smiling on the outside but hurting on the inside. There is something missing. Proverbs 14:13 addresses this: "Even in laughter, the heart may ache." For many, what is missing is a personal and saving relationship with Jesus Christ.[24]

Reaching People

I look for the truth of God wherever I go, and sometimes I find it in the most unexpected places—like a fast-food restaurant. Let me explain. A few years ago, the executives of a fast-food chain noticed something that greatly concerned them. Over a period of years, their restaurant had shown steady growth, but then suddenly, out of the blue, there came a point where their sales plateaued. Alarmed, they called together their brightest minds to address this problem. This think tank of top executives concluded that they needed to get back to the basics by asking: "Who are our customers? Who are we trying to serve? Whom are we trying to reach with our product?"

The answer that they eventually decided on wasthis: "Whoever comes into our restaurants." With that answer in hand, they developed a survey to gain insight from the people who dined with them. They asked questions such as, "Do you want your food like this or like that?" They compiled the survey information and went to work implementing the changes the customers suggested. They expected to see a swift, upward trend in sales. But it didn't happen. Sales stayed flat.

The company again summoned their brain trust to take a second look at the problem. They decided they had asked the right question: "Who are our customers?" The answer to which they came, however, apparently was wrong! The second time around, they concluded the answer was, "Anybody who eats!"

They came to the conclusion they weren't just trying to reach people who came to their restaurants, but rather, they were trying to reach anyone who gets hungry!

So they asked another question: "Where do people get hungry?" Answer: "At shopping malls, at sporting events, at travel centers . . . " With that answer they broke out of the box that had them trapped and prevented their moving upward in sales. Now, it seems, everywhere you look, you see units of this fast-food chain. They have taken their product out to where people get hungry—airports, shopping malls, discount stores, convenience stores, college campuses, and even ballparks. As a result, their sales have risen.

What does this have to do with the Lord's church? The question those young executives asked is a question we, the church, should also be asking. "Whom are we trying to reach?" We should ask, "Who are we trying to serve?" The answer should be much the same as theirs. It is not just those who come within our walls, but rather anybody who gets hungry for the gospel, the good news of Jesus Christ. And that "anybody" is everybody!

We should take the gracious, loving, caring ministry of Jesus out of the church buildings and to a lost and hungry world. Perhaps no one has answered this important question more accurately than John Wesley when he said, "The world is our parish!"[25]

Surrender

Some time ago there was an Associated Press article in the newspaper about a Japanese soldier who refused to accept Japan's surrender. He remained on a tiny Philippine island for twenty-nine years after the end of World War II. Trained as an intelligence officer, former army Lt. Hiroo Onoda had been sent in December 1944 to Lubang, a tiny island ninety miles southwest of Manila, with orders to spy on the U.S. military. He refused to believe Japan had surrendered when American forces landed on Lubang in 1945, remaining in hiding in the jungle until 1974.

After the war ended, Onoda and two other soldiers who remained with him occasionally skirmished with local villagers and Filipino troops. Finally on March 10, 1974, Onoda, dressed in his imperial army uniform, stepped out of the jungle to receive the order to stop fighting from his former superior, who had traveled to the Philippines to deliver the message.

Onoda is like many people who refuse to surrender their sins and their lives to the conquering Lord Jesus. They continue to resist the One who has come to emancipate them from oppression. Once they lay down their sins and their pride, they will find the new Ruler of their hearts to be a loving and forgiving God who liberates them to a new life of freedom and peace.

Sin

All Sin

There are millions of people today who would deny their guilt before God. They're "sincere, honest, good people." But the words of Paul in the letter to the Romans ring out: "All have sinned and fall short of the glory of God."

Andy got up late one morning and wasn't ready for the test in his first class. As he walked down the hall on the way to class, he spotted the professor coming toward him. In that moment, he decided to cut the class, so he ducked into the rest room. In a few seconds, the door opened, and in walked the professor. Andy wasn't as concerned about cutting the class as he was in discovering he was standing with this professor in the ladies' room!

You may try to avoid responsibility for your actions, but "your sins will find you out." Recognize that each of us stands justly accused before a righteous God. We have sinned, and we deserve to be condemned. Then reach out and accept the offer of free and full pardon from a Christ who loves you and who gave His life for you.[26]

Cost of Unchecked Sin

For eight years Sally had been the Romero family pet. When they got her, she was only one foot long. Sally grew, however, until she eventually reached eleven-and-a-half feet and weighed eighty pounds. Then on July 20, 1993, Sally, a Burmese python, turned on fifteen-year-old Derek, strangling the teenager until he died of suffocation. Associated Press Online (7/22/93) quoted the police as saying that the snake was "quite aggressive, hissing, and reacting" when they arrived to investigate. Sins that seem little and harmless will grow. Tolerate or ignore sin, and it will eventually lead to death (see James 1:15).[27]

Effects of Unchecked Sin

On the western slopes of the Rocky Mountains, a giant Sequoia tree lies rotting. It was a growing sapling when Christ walked the shores of the Sea of Galilee. When Columbus discovered America, it was reaching maturity; it looked down from lofty heights during the American Civil War. It withstood the ravages of fires, floods, storms, and droughts. It seemed destined to live many more centuries.

Then, a few years ago, a tiny beetle started to burrow into its bark and lay the eggs that would produce other beetles. It seemed like an unequal battle at first, but the few beetles multiplied into hundreds, then thousands, and finally millions. First they attacked the bark, then they worked deeper and deeper into the trunk, and finally, they were eating at the very heart and strength of that magnificent forest giant.

Then one day—after withstanding the elements for centuries—the rains came, the winds blew, the lightning flashed, and the giant sequoia fell—but not because of the elements. It fell because of the weakening effect of those tiny beetles. Bad habits do the same to people. They slowly take a toll until the day comes when the man, like the tree, falls.[28]

Sin's Eggs

How does a worm get inside an apple? Perhaps you think the worm burrows in from the outside. No, scientists have discovered that the worm comes from the inside. But how does it get in there? Simple! An insect lays an egg in the apple blossom. Sometime later, the worm hatches in the heart of the apple, then eats his way out. Sin, like the worm, begins in the heart and works out through a person's thoughts, words, and actions. For this reason, David once wrote, "Create in me a clean heart, O God" (Ps. 51:10, KJV).[29]

Toxic Cleanup

How to dispose of toxic wastes is one of the most difficult dilemmas in modern American life. Indeed, some experts consider chemical poisons the world's biggest problem next to nuclear bombs. The difference is that tons of deadly compounds are already seeping into our soil and water, but not a single atomic warhead has yet been exploded outside of government control in our country. Toxic wastes improperly stored are "ticking away like time bombs" in tens of thousands of landfills and water sources across our country.

Mankind is very good at producing not only a high level of *physical* toxins that endanger the body, but also a high level of *spiritual* toxins that imperil the soul. Furthermore, just as our flesh requires a clean atmosphere to ensure health, so, too, our hearts must be cleansed of those deadly sins that contaminate.

Where is the answer to this problem of toxicity to be found? The gospel points us to "the Lamb of God, who takes away the sin of the world" through the Cross (John 1:29) and whose shed blood "purifies us" from all contamination (1 John 1:7, 9). Calvary made forever clear that our sins are truly "toxic"—death-dealing both for Christ and for us, but Easter announces that he took those toxic wastes to the tomb and left them there![30]

CHAPTER ELEVEN

The Exaltation

❖

One of the most powerful and meaningful experiences in celebrating the Lord's Table is the opportunity to express our feelings and thoughts through the medium of music. The following is a list of hymns, choruses, and "specials" that can be used in services of communion.

Atonement/Blood of Christ

An asterisk (*) denotes solo/ensemble/choir selection

Alas! and Did My Savior Bleed?
Are You Washed in the Blood?
By Your Blood (Integrity Music/Christensen)
I Believe in Jesus (Mercy Pub./Nelson)
**Calvary* (Word Music/Cymbala)
Glory to His Name
**God's Sacrifice* (Havudidju Pub./Switzer)
Hallelujah, What a Savior!
Jesus Paid It All
Jesus, Thy Blood and Righteousness
Lamb of Glory (Meadowgreen Songs/Nelson/McHugh)

Man of Sorrows
*My Cross (Integrity Music/Christensen)
My Tribute (CMI/Crouch)
Nothing but the Blood
O, the Blood of Jesus (Word Music/Unknown)
*Oh the Blood (Luminar Music/Harper)
*Redeemed (What's Music/Chadwick)
Rock of Ages
*Saved (JaTwon/Kee)
The Blood Will Never Lose Its Power (Manna Music/Crouch)
*The Story (Royal Tapestry/arr. Clydesdale)
The Strong Name of Jesus (Maranatha
        Music/Cloninger/Chapman)
There Is a Green Hill Far Away
There Is Power in the Blood
There Is a Redeemer (Sparrow Corp./Green)
To God Be the Glory

Christ's Passion/Christ's Love for Us

And Can It Be
Because He Lives (Wm. Gaither/Gaither/Gaither)
Blessed Redeemer
Everlasting Light (Word Music/Cloninger/Hayes)
For the Lord is Good (Integrity Music/Funk)
*How Beautiful (Ariose Music/Paris)
How Jesus Loves (Word Music/Cymbala)
I Gave My Life for Thee
**Isn't He?* (Mercy Publishing/Wimber)
O How He Loves You and Me

O How I Love Jesus
O How Deep, How Broad, How High
O Sacred Head, Now Wounded
Oh, How He Loves You and Me (Word Music/Kaiser)
Thanks!
There Is a Fountain
Think about His Love (Integrity Music/Harrah)
'Tis Midnight—And on Olive's Brow
We Remember You (Maranatha Music/arr. Marestaing)
Were You There?
Jesus Loves Me

Cleansing/Forgiveness

A Perfect Heart (CMI/McGuire/Rambo)
All That You Need (Word Music/Cymbala)
Create in Me a Clean Heart
I Believe in Jesus (Mercy Pub./Nelson)
Jesus, I Come
Jesus, Lover of My Soul
Whiter than Snow
You Are My All in All (Shepherd's Heart/Jernigan)

Commitment

All For Jesus
Breathe on Me, Breath of God
Change My Heart, O God (Mercy Publishing/Expinosa)
Come to the River of Life (Integrity Music/Moen/Cloninger)
Fill My Cup, Lord

Have Thine Own Way
I Am Thine, O Lord
I Have Decided to Follow Jesus
I Surrender All
I'd Rather Have Jesus
I'll Live for Him
In My Life, Lord, Be Glorified (Kilpatrick Music/Kilpatrick)
Jesus, Jesus (Word Music/Bullock)
*Jesus, Rock of Ages (Word Music/Cymbala)
Lead On, O King Eternal
Living for Jesus
Must Jesus Bear the Cross Alone
Open Our Eyes, Lord (Maranatha Music/Cull)
Something for Thee
Take My Life and Let It Be
Take Up Your Cross (Shepherd Boy Music/Millikan)
We Dedicate This Time to You (Integrity Music/Kenoly)
When I Survey the Wondrous Cross
Where He Leads Me
Wherever He Leads I'll Go

Cross of Christ

At Calvary
At the Cross
Beneath the Cross of Jesus
Draw Me Nearer
In the Cross
Lead Me to Calvary
Near the Cross

Room at the Cross for Me
The Old Rugged Cross
To the Cross (Word Music/Adams/Mason)
When He Was on the Cross (Wind in Willow Pub./Hinson/Payne)
When I Survey the Wondrous Cross

Grace

Amazing Grace
But for Grace (Integrity Music/Baroni/Chisum)
Come, Thou Fount
Grace, Greater Than Our Sin
Touch of Grace (Integrity Music/Kerr/Searcy)
When All Thy Mercies
Wonderful Grace of Jesus

Miscellaneous

Blest Be the Tie
Bread of the World
*Communion Medley (Word Music/arr. Cymbala)
Let Us Break Bread Together on Our Knees

Praise and Worship

All Hail, King Jesus (Tempo Music Pub./Moody)
Alleluia (Manna Music/Sinclair)
As the Deer (Maranatha Music/Nystrom)
Celebrate Jesus (Integrity Music/Oliver)
Glorify Thy Name (Maranatha Music/Adkins)

Glory to the Lamb (Zion Song Music/Dempsey)
He Is Lord (Word Music/Traditional)
His Name Is Wonderful (Manna Music/Mieir)
Holy Ground (Meadowgreen Music/Davis)
Holy, Holy (CMI/Owens)
Holy, Holy, Holy
How Excellent Is Thy Name (Word Music/Tunney)
I Exalt Thee (Pete Sanchez Jr./Sanchez)
I Love You, Lord (Maranatha/Klein)
I Will Celebrate (Maranatha Music/Baloche)
I Worship You, Almighty God (Integrity Music/Corbett)
Jesus Is Alive (Integrity Music/Kenoly)
Jesus, Draw Me Close (Maranatha Music/Founds)
Jesus, Lover of My Soul (Integrity Music/Ezzy/Grul/McPherson)
Jesus, Name above All Names (Maranatha/Hearn)
King of Kings (Maranatha Music/Conty/Batya)
Lift High the Lord, Our Banner (Integrity Music/Delavan)
Lord, I Lift Your Name on High (Maranatha Music/Founds)
Majesty (Rocksmith Music/Hayford)
My Life Is in You, Lord (Integrity Music/Gardner)
No Other Name (Integrity Music/Gay)
O, Come Let Us Adore Him
Oh, How I Love Jesus (Word Music/arr. Cymbala)
Oh, the Glory of Your Presence (EMI Christian Music/Fry)
Praise the Name of Jesus (Sparrowith/Hicks)
Shout to the Lord (Integrity Music/Shout to the Lord/Zschech)
There's Something about That Name
    (Wm. Gaither/Gaither/Gaither)
We Will Glorify (Singspiration Music/Paris)
Worthy of Worship (McKinney Press/Blankenship/York)

We Will Worship (Shepherd's Heart/Jernigan)
You Are Worthy to Be Praised (RCM Enterprises/Cook)

Thanksgiving

Come, Ye Thankful People, Come
Great Is Thy Faithfulness
The Lamb Has Overcome (Word Music/Cymbala)
We Gather Together

CHAPTER TWELVE

The Citation

───────── ❖ ─────────

I t is crucial to examine multiple passages of scripture when preparing a sermon. Looking at what God's Word has to say about a given topic throughout the Testaments yields rich insight. As I prepare a meditation on the Lord's Supper, I prayerfully open His Word and seek the Spirit's fresh teaching on this sacred feast. A small "concordance" of passages related to the Lord's Supper which may be helpful in studying His Word follows.

Cross/Death of Christ

Isaiah 53:1–12
3 He was despised and rejected by men, a man of sorrows, and familiar with suffering.

4 He took up our infirmities and carried our sorrows.

5 He was pierced for our transgressions, he was crushed for our iniquities.

7 He was oppressed and afflicted . . . led like a lamb to the slaughter.

9 He was assigned a grave.

[10] It was the LORD's will to crush him and cause him to suffer.

Matthew 16:21 (See also Matt. 17:22–23, 20:17–19, 26:2; Mark 8:31, 10:32–34; Luke 9:22, 18:31–33)

[21] Jesus began to explain to his disciples that he must go to Jerusalem and . . . be killed.

Matthew 27:33–37 (See also John 19:36)

[35] When they had crucified him, they divided up his clothes by casting lots.

Matthew 27:46 (See also Ps. 22:1)

[46] "My God, my God, why have you forsaken me?"

John 10:11

[11] "I am the good shepherd. The good shepherd lays down his life for the sheep."

John 10:15–18

[17] "I lay down my life."

[18] "No one takes it from me, but I lay it down of my own accord."

John 12:32–33

[32] "When I am lifted up . . . [I] will draw all men to myself."

John 14:19

[19] "Before long, the world will not see me anymore."

John 19:28–30

[28] "I am thirsty."

[30] "It is finished."

John 19:36

³⁶ "Not one of his bones will be broken."

Acts 26:22–23

²³ Christ would suffer.

1 Corinthians 1:17–18

¹⁸ The message of the cross is foolishness . . . it is the power of God.

1 Corinthians 15:3–4

³ Christ died for our sins according to the Scriptures.

1 Thessalonians 4:14

¹⁴ Jesus died and rose again.

Revelation 5:12

¹² Worthy is the Lamb, who was slain.

Design/Purpose of Christ's Death

Isaiah 53:1–12

⁵ For our transgressions . . . for our iniquities . . . brought us peace . . . we are healed.

⁸ For the transgression.

¹⁰ A guilt offering . . . the will of the Lord will prosper in his hand.

¹¹ Will justify many . . . bear their iniquities.

¹² For he bore the sin of many . . . made intercession.

Matthew 20:28

²⁸ "To give his life as a ransom for many."

Matthew 26:28

[28] "This is my blood . . . poured out for many for the forgiveness of sins."

John 3:14–17

[15] "May have eternal life."

[16] "Shall not perish but have eternal life."

[17] "To save the world through him."

John 6:51

[51] "This bread is my flesh, which I will give for the life of the world."

John 11:49–52

[51] Jesus would die for the Jewish nation.

[52] Also for the scattered children of God.

John 12:24

[24] Produces many seeds.

John 12:31–33

[32] "Will draw all men to myself."

Acts 5:30–31

[31] That he might give repentance and forgiveness.

Romans 3:24–25

[25] A sacrifice of atonement . . . to demonstrate his justice.

Romans 4:25

[25] For our justification.

Romans 5:6–11

[6] Died for the ungodly.

⁹ Justified by his blood . . . saved from God's wrath.
¹⁰ We were reconciled to him.

Romans 6:3–5

⁴ We too may live a new life.
⁵ Be united with him in his resurrection.

Romans 8:3

³ To be a sin offering.

Romans 8:32

³² Graciously give us all things.

2 Corinthians 4:10–11

¹⁰ That the life of Jesus may also be revealed in our body.

2 Corinthians 5:14–21

¹⁵ That those who live should no longer live for themselves.
¹⁷ A new creation.
¹⁸ Reconciled us to himself.
²¹ In him we might become the righteousness of God.

Galatians 2:20

²⁰ Christ lives in me.

Ephesians 1:4–7

⁴ For he chose us in him . . . to be holy and blameless.
⁵ Predestined us to be adopted as his sons.
⁷ Have redemption through his blood.

Ephesians 2:13–16

¹³ Brought near through the blood of Christ.
¹⁴ Destroyed the barrier.

[15] To create in himself one new man.

[16] To reconcile both of them.

Colossians 1:20–22

[20] To reconcile to himself all things.

[22] To present you holy in his sight.

1 Thessalonians 5:9–10

[9] To receive salvation.

[10] May live together with him.

Titus 2:13–14

[14] To redeem us from all wickedness and to purify.

Hebrews 2:9–10

[9] He might taste death for everyone.

Hebrews 2:14

[14] He might destroy . . . the devil.

Hebrews 9:12–17

[12] Having obtained eternal redemption.

[13] So that they are outwardly clean.

[14] Cleanse our consciences . . . so that we may serve the living God!

[15] May receive the promised eternal inheritance.

Hebrews 10:12

[12] One sacrifice for sins.

Hebrews 12:2–3

[3] So that you will not grow weary and lose heart.

1 Peter 1:18–21
²¹ So your faith and hope are in God.

1 Peter 2:24
²⁴ So that we might die to sins and live for righteousness . . . have been healed.

1 Peter 3:18
¹⁸ For sins once for all.

1 John 1:7
⁷ We have fellowship one with another . . . purifies us from all sin.

1 John 2:2
² The atoning sacrifice for our sins.

The Blood

Exodus 12:7–23
⁷ Then they are to take some of the blood and put it on the sides and tops of the doorframes.
¹¹ It is the LORD's Passover.
¹³ The blood will be a sign for you . . . I will pass over.
²¹ Go . . . and slaughter the Passover lamb.
²² Take a bunch of hyssop, dip it into the blood.

John 6:53–56
⁵⁴ "Whoever eats my flesh and drinks my blood has eternal life."

John 19:34
³⁴ Soldiers pierced Jesus' side . . . blood.

Romans 3:24–25
²⁵ A sacrifice of atonement . . . his blood.

Romans 5:8–9
⁹ Justified by his blood.

1 Corinthians 10:16
¹⁶ Cup of thanksgiving . . . participation in the body of Christ.

Ephesians 1:7
⁷ Redemption through his blood.

Ephesians 2:13
¹³ Brought near through the blood of Christ.

Hebrews 9:12–14
¹² He entered the Most Holy Place once for all by his own blood.
¹⁴ The blood of Christ . . . cleanse our consciences from acts that lead to death.

Hebrews 9:22
²² Without the shedding of blood there is no forgiveness.

Hebrews 10:19–20
¹⁹ We have confidence to enter the Most Holy Place by the blood of Jesus.

Hebrews 13:11–12

¹² Jesus also suffered . . . to make the people holy through his own blood.

1 Peter 1:18–19

¹⁹ The precious blood of Christ, a lamb without blemish or defect.

1 John 1:7

⁷ The blood of Jesus, his Son, purifies us from all sin.

Revelation 1:5–6

⁵ Freed us from our sins by his blood.

Revelation 5:9

9 With your blood you purchased men for God.

Prophecies of Christ's Suffering

Psalm 22:6–8

⁶ Scorned by men and despised.
⁷ Mock me.

Psalm 22:11–13

¹¹ Trouble is near.
¹² Many bulls surround me.
¹³ Roaring lions . . . open their mouths wide against me.

Psalm 22:17–18

¹⁷ I can count all my bones; people stare and gloat over me.
¹⁸ They divide my garments among them and cast lots for my clothing.

Matthew 27:35 (See also Mark 15:24; Luke 23:34)

[35] When they had crucified him, they divided up his clothes by casting lots.

Psalm 69:7–9

[7] I endure scorn for your sake.

[8] I am a stranger to my brothers.

Psalm 109:25

[25] I am an object of scorn to my accusers.

Isaiah 50:6

[16] I offered my back to those who beat me . . . I did not hide my face from mocking and spitting.

Isaiah 53:2–12

[3] He was despised and rejected by men, a man of sorrows, and familiar with suffering.

[4] He took up our infirmities and carried our sorrows.

[5] But he was pierced for our transgressions, he was crushed for our iniquities; the punishment . . . was upon him, and by his wounds we are healed.

[7] He was led like a lamb to the slaughter.

[8] By oppression and judgment he was taken away.

[9] He was assigned a grave with the wicked.

[10] It was the LORD's will to crush him and cause him to suffer.

[11] After the suffering of his soul . . . he will bear their iniquities.

[12] He poured out his life unto death.

Luke 22:37

[37] "It is written: 'And he was numbered with the transgressors'; and I tell you that this must be fulfilled in me. Yes, what is written about me is reaching its fulfillment."

Luke 18:31–33 (See also Mark 10:32–34)

³¹ Jesus took the Twelve aside and told them, "We are going up to Jerusalem, and everything that is written by the prophets about the Son of Man will be fulfilled.

³² "He will be handed over to the Gentiles. They will mock him, insult him, spit on him, flog him and kill him."

Messianic Psalms

Psalm 2:1–12

⁶ "I have installed my King on Zion, my holy hill."

⁷ I will proclaim the decree of the LORD: He said to me, "You are my Son."

Psalm 16:7–11

⁹ My body also will rest secure.

¹⁰ because you will not abandon me to the grave, nor will you let your Holy One see decay.

¹¹ You have made known to me the path of life; you will fill me with joy in your presence, with eternal pleasures at your right hand.

Psalm 72:1–19

¹ The royal son.

² Will judge your people in righteousness.

⁴ He will crush the oppressor.

⁵ He will endure as long as the sun, as long as the moon, through all generations.

⁸ He will rule . . . to the ends of the earth.

¹¹ All kings will bow down to him and all nations will serve him.

[12] For he will deliver.

[17] All nations will be blessed through him, and they will call him blessed.

Psalm 96:1–13

[2] Sing to the LORD, praise his name; proclaim his salvation day after day.

[13] He comes to judge the earth. He will judge the world in righteousness and the peoples in his truth.

Psalm 118:19–29

[22] The stone the builders rejected has become the capstone.

Contributed by William F. Mitchell
First Baptist Church, Orlando, Florida

Notes

❖

1. Wayne Grudem, *Systematic Theology* (Grand Rapids: Zondervan, 1994), 989–91.

2. William Evans, *The Great Doctrines of the Bible* (Chicago: Moody Press, 1976), 304.

3. Adapted from Winward and Cox, *Worship Manual* (Asheville, N.C.: World, 1969), 14.

4. Philip P. Bliss, *Hallelujah, What a Savior!*

5. Warren Wiersbe, *Be Wise* (Wheaton: Victor Books, 1984), 113–18.

6. Source unknown.

7. Paul Brand and Philip Yancey, "Blood: The Miracle of Cleansing, Part One," *Christianity Today,* 18 Feb. 1983, 13–14.

8. Ibid., 15.

9. Ibid.

10. John Killinger, "What God Was Saying at the Cross," *Preaching,* July–Aug., 1988, 17.

11. Leon Morris, "More Than a Symbol," *Christianity Today,* 17 Apr. 1987, 23.

12. David B. Davis, Dynamics for Living, Pearland, Tex.

13. Myrtice Smith, *Alive Forevermore!* 5.

14. Derric Johnson, "The Trees," published by Derric Johnson Press and used by permission.

15. Ibid.

16. Steve Brown, "Forgiven and Forgotten," *Key Life,* Mar./Apr., 1990, 2.

17. Philip Yancey, "Are We Asking Too Much?" *Christianity Today,* 22 Nov. 1985, 30.

16. Kay D. Rizzo, "The Presidential Pardon," *Signs of the Times,* Nov. 1996, 21.

17. Robert Dickson, Hope Presbyterian Church, Richfield, Minn..

20. W. Loyd Allen, "Crucial Forgiveness," *Preaching,* Mar./Apr., 1991, 22.

21. Doug Jackson, First Baptist Church, Fountain Hills, Ariz., newsletter.

22. *Daily Bread.*

23. From *The Sword of the Lord* (31 May 1996), 11, 14.

24. Source unknown.

25. J. Howard Edington, *The Whole World in His Hands,* First Presbyterian Church, Orlando, Fla., 6 Oct. 1996. Used by permission.

26. Harold C. Perdue, Sam Wilson, Michael Duduit, "Who's to Blame?" *Preaching,* July–Aug. 1986, 41.

27. Bruce E. Truman, Mt. Olivet, Ky.

28. Zig Ziglar, *See You at the Top,* (Pelican Publishing, 1975).

29. From *Sword of the Lord* (November, 1996).

30. William E. Hull, "Where Shall We Dump Our Toxic Wastes?" *Church Chimes* (Shreveport, La.: First Baptist Church, 4 Sept. 1983), 3.